BLACK BOY
FROM THE
BARRIO

Cornelius Wright

PAGE PUBLISHING, INC.
Conneaut Lake, PA

First originally published by Page Publishing 2021

ISBN 978-1-64334-804-9 (pbk)
ISBN 978-1-64334-803-2 (digital)

Printed in the United States of America

DEDICATION

I would like to dedicate all my books to the following three people. I am sure there will be dedications and shoutouts for other important people as well as I continue to write for the remainder of my life. However, these three "primary people" and the positive influence that they have had in my life is dyed into the fabric of my existence. As long as I am living, they will never be forgotten.

Dorothy Wright

This wonderful woman is my mother. She is the epitome of living life to the fullest and not letting the struggles of life change her outlook on living a positive and fulfilling life. I will not go into depth about her life now; however, I will be telling many stories of her brave and fascinating life in future chapters. Stricken with schizophrenia at a young age, I will explain how she coped with this serious mental illness during a time when having a mental illness was truly stigmatized. During that time (the 1960s), countless people were sent to mental institutions and given procedures and medications that were not proven to be effective. Luckily, science and medicine have come a long way since those days; however, when dealing with the complexities of the human brain, there is still much to learn. Dorothy Wright, aka Mama, is now eighty-four years old and is living at a care facility in the Central Valley. Although her schizophrenia still needs to be managed by high a dosage of psychotic medications, her incredible positive attitude has still remained with her. She is truly an inspiration to me and will be forever in my heart. I love you, Mama. Way to go!

Now that I am a mental health advocate, and having to live with my own mental illness since 2017, I will be starting a nonprofit in her honor called the Dorothy Wright Foundation in which a generous portion of all my earnings (starting with the sale of my first book) will be donated to giving money to charity and bringing awareness to mental illness on a large scale.

I truly believe that most things happen for a reason. I think that struggling with a mental illness on a daily basis has taught me so much of what true life is all about. The first thing that comes to mind is to not take things for granted. For so many years, especially in my youth, I lived life as though I was going to live forever. Fortunately, over twenty years ago, I started making some drastic changes in the way that I think that still impacts my life in a positive way. By becoming a certified life coach, author, and speaker, I now have the proper platform to reach countless people worldwide that are in need.

Clemetie Wright

Clemetie Wright was not only my father but he was also a man that I looked up to, especially at a young age. Not only was he a hard worker but he was also a family man as well. He was very instrumental in keeping our family unit together when our mother was experiencing psychotic episodes during most of her life. His undying love and patience got our family through some very challenging times when we were kids. Although he had some faults (like we all do), I have never held any of his past mistakes against him. He admitted to me many times that he made some mistakes in his life that he was not very proud of, especially when he was young. By admitting this, he reminded me that none of us are perfect and that we are all human. Daddy passed away at the tender age of sixty-six in 1997 from lung cancer. I still think about him a lot, and I don't want him to be forgotten. As long as I am living, Daddy, I promise you that you will not be forgotten. Good job, Daddy. You da man. Way to go!

John (Wing Hing) Papa Doc Wong

The third person that I would like to dedicate my books to is my father in-law, John Wong aka Papa Doc. Papa Doc was not only brilliant as far as IQ but he was also a very intriguing man, to say the least. He was a true Renaissance man who was involved in many interesting endeavors. He was very instrumental in me writing this book. From a standpoint of achievement, I don't know or haven't met anyone in my lifetime that has accomplished as much as he did. I don't believe that anyone should live a life just to accomplish things and to impress others. He accomplished these things because they made him happy. Some of the things he accomplished were as follows:

1. Physician (over fifty years)
2. Studied law
3. Fencing expert
4. Guitar player
5. Accomplished piano player
6. Accomplished painter (portraits)
7. Real estate investor
8. World traveler
9. Author

He was the epitome of success, life, and what true happiness should entail. How do I know this? Because I asked him. Shortly before he died, I had a conversation with him on one of our "man trips" to the Home Depot. I asked him a very intriguing question that most people would try to avoid. I asked him if he'd had a chance to change anything in his life thus far, what would it be? With one of his famous chuckles, he said, "If I could change anything in my previous life, I would have eaten more caviar and escargot."

"Is that it?" I said in a stunned voice. Of course, by now, I know that he was kidding around. He told me that he could not wait to go into his office and visit his patients. He loved what he did. He was the first person that I met that had no regrets from the life he lived. I am trying my best to be able to say those words when my time comes. Papa Doc will be mentioned plenty in upcoming books. Unfortunately, Papa Doc passed away in the summer of 2014. He was eighty-three years old at the time and had obviously lived a very fulfilled life. Way to go, Papa Doc!

Preface

Thinking. What a dangerous pastime. I am sitting at Starbucks in North Berkeley on this foggy morning in July 2015, thinking about what to write about in a book about my life. Now, why on earth would I want to do something like this anyway? What would a fifty-four-year-old African American man that has never read a book from cover to cover until he was thirty-one years old and was a house painter for thirty-two years plus only has a high school education have to say that would not only interest people but also possibly inspire them? My answer to that question would be "plenty." I was once told by someone that every human being has a book in them. Also, I was told "to whom much is given, much is expected." Trust me, I have been given a lot. Now, it's time for me to give back.

It is now August 2019, and I am completing my memoirs on the first of a series of books entitled *Black Boy from the Barrio*. I just looked at my notes from 2015, and I can see that I gave myself a five-year time frame to finish volume one. I will actually get it done a year ahead of schedule. Way to go, Cornelius!

Looking back on my life now, I realize that there has always been a part of me that was considered by many to be a little different. What I mean by that is that ever since I was a little boy, I have always had dreams of doing something big or being someone of significance. I can't explain why; it has just been that way for me ever since I can remember. I have this inner drive that I now believe is a gift from God. As I have gotten older and realized this special gift, ignoring it would be a travesty, as far as I am concerned. I decided to start writing because I think this is the best way to connect to people in a way that spoken words can't. By the way, everything that I write about is for the betterment of humankind. So when I write, I write with purpose and I put my whole heart and soul into it. I realize that some of the things that I write about will turn some people off while other things will inspire them. I wish that I could influence everyone in a positive way, but I know that's impossible.

Also, I have decided that writing is a lifelong project for me. I will write both short stories and long stories that will be inspirational, humorous, and with great storylines and plots. I will write children's books as well as books on business and personal development. I also have a strong spiritual connection that has given me direction when I hit some of the "valleys of life." So I will try to connect to as many people on that level as well. I have an array of interesting subjects and knowledge about the many facets of life that we humans face on a daily basis. How? Because I have lived it and continue (thank you, Lord) to live it on a daily basis. Fifty-eight years on this planet has taught me a lot; however, I feel that I have just gotten started. I invite you to take this journey with me as I continue to grow and find the true meaning of my life and possibly you can find the meaning of yours as well.

Sincerely,
Cornelius

"Hi, I am Neo. Nice to meet you."

Those simple little words have allowed me to meet many fascinating people during my lifetime. When I meet them for the first time, I look directly into their eyes and spout those words. Maybe I am a country boy from the barrio and the "old school," but this is the way that I was taught. I think this is a good way not only to break the initial ice but also to show warmth and sincerity that the other person usually appreciates. Realizing that we will be spending a lot of time getting to know one another, I thought that this would be a good gesture to start our relationship that will hopefully last for many years to come.

The name Neo is just a nickname that was given to me by my family at a young age because Cornelius was just too hard to pronounce by a lot of people. Actually, my nickname is not Neo. My brothers and sisters still call me Neeyo. Neo is the version that I started calling myself when I moved to Berkeley and started hanging around people that were mainly brilliant UC Berkeley students. I wanted to fit in, so I decided that Neo sounded cool. To be honest with you, it sounded "white." I am not saying that all white people and all black people speak in a certain way, of course, but I think you know what I mean. Maybe I should restate this and just say that Neo is the proper way in which to say the ghetto version of the name, which is Neeyo.

Anyway, it worked! They were impressed, and I felt good that I was clever enough to get them to acknowledge me. I still get many compliments on my nickname. Of course, when I went back to the hood where my family was living, I was Neeyo again. Then, they came out with the movie *The Matrix*. What a can of worms that opened. Some people started to think I named myself after the character Neo in that movie. I tell them no, of course. But, I wouldn't mind receiving some fat royalty checks from that great series of movies (good luck with that, right?). However, I don't think that I ever will because the only thing that we (both Neos) have in common is our names. He is a white computer whiz who thinks he is superman and is called the One, and I am a nontech black kid from the barrio that, at certain times in my life, could be called the None.

I was also called a plethora of names that came from Cornelius. Many of my friends from Delano and Earlimart know me as Corny. I was also called Corn, Corndog, Cornball, and in some cases, Cornsh#t from various people that were mad at me. Trust me, by the time I finish this series of books, you will know me very well, which is my intent. Hopefully, I will get to know many of you as well.

7/9/2015

Getting to Know the Author

I am writing these opening words so that my audience and I can have an intimate, trusting, and honest relationship that will last over time. I have always valued good relationships and have held them in high regard. As an author, I am trying to get my audience to understand what makes me tick and how I see the world. However, it's not all about me, right? My goal is to give my audience something that can enhance their lives in a positive way by making them think in a way that they may have not thought about previously. I have a saying that I once heard that goes something like this, "We are not human beings, we are human becomings."

I realize that this sort of talk makes some people want to vomit in their mouths. (Yuck!) I also understand that we humans are not all the same. But I can promise you that we are much more alike than we are different. I also have discovered over time that all of us humans have flaws. As a certified life coach, I have been studying human nature for a while now. What I have found out is that although we all have flaws, there is nothing WRONG with us. Most of us, including myself, have spent almost an entire lifetime trying to FIX ourselves when we don't need fixing at all. This is the way we were made, and we should be proud of that.

I am learning to accept myself as I am through certain practices that I will talk about later. Stay tuned because, hopefully, it can be as life-changing for you as it has been for me. I believe that we were all instilled with a brain that allows us to dream and to want the best lives for ourselves and possibly for our loved ones as well. I am a follower of Christ because of his principles of unconditional love. I try hard to live by these principles daily in order to become a better person; however, I am a work in progress, so hopefully, you guys will be patient with me. By being human, I will undoubtedly say some things that not all people will agree with. However, I will promise you that whatever I do in this life, it is to glorify God and to have a positive impact on humankind.

If what I am writing about so far is boring to you or might make you feel uncomfortable in some kind of way, then perhaps this book is not for you. That's perfectly okay with me. However, as humans, the only way in which we grow is through getting out of our comfort zones. I know this firsthand because, for countless years in my youth, I tried my best to stay within the safe confines of my comfort zone. It did not work out so well for me, as I will discuss in upcoming chapters. So perhaps reading this might be just what the doctor ordered for you. I sincerely hope that it will be.

UNCONVENTIONAL OPENING WORDS

I have read many books in the past twenty-five years. However, before the age of thirty-one, I had not read an entire book from cover to cover. I read textbooks at school because it was required to pass the class. While growing up on a farm and, eventually, the barrio, our family were not readers. We would watch television and play outside. My oldest sister is now an avid reader, but I don't remember her reading much when she was a child either. My point is that I can't remember reading a book where the author is purposely trying to "communicate" to his readers in the way that I am. I could be wrong (not the first time and definitely not the last time) but I can't recall any book that I have read thus far where the author is trying to connect so openly. I think by letting my readers know what I am trying to achieve, there won't be any grey areas in our relationships.

I think, as humans, the best communication comes when we allow ourselves to be vulnerable. I used to think that being vulnerable is a weakness, especially growing up as a male in our society. It has taken me countless years of growth to finally break some of the stifling and destructive stereotypes that are placed upon us men. I continue to work every day to become a better human being and try to understand how I fit in, what's my purpose, and what I can do to change the world. "Change the world?" you might ask! I realize that many people can't begin to even fathom words like those. But I am here to tell you that I can, with God's help of course. Understanding this makes just about anything possible, if you BELIEVE it.

Breaking Barriers

If you guys don't mind, I would like to spend a little time writing about why I am doing what I do. One of the most important parts of my journey is breaking barriers. Let me explain. As far as I know, in the history of my family, no one has broken some very important barriers that could continue to be a burden on future generations. I decided years ago to take on this incredibly hard task because not only is it necessary for me personally but it can also alter the course of our family's history. So what I am embarking on is much bigger than me. For some reason, God gave me the courage, resilience, and vision to attempt such an endeavor. I will be explaining what barriers I am talking about shortly. These same barriers have plagued countless families and millions upon millions of people.

The first barrier that I would like to talk about is the alcohol barrier. It can also be called the substance abuse barrier, but since alcohol was the main one in my family's heritage, I will stick to that. Like many families, alcohol consumption was and still is a major problem. It's more than just a family problem; it's a worldwide human problem. Now, don't get me wrong, I am not talking about people who drink in a social way. Drinking in moderation can be fun and a good way to socialize. In many societies, drinking alcohol is a way of life. So I am not saying to ban alcohol. I believe that just about anything has a certain place in our society, including alcohol.

The point that I am trying to make here is how alcohol affected my family since I came into existence. I won't go into much detail now, because I will be telling stories in later chapters about how it had a negative effect, not only in my life, but my predecessors as well.

The second barrier that I am attempting to break is the "Poverty" barrier. I realize that the word poverty can mean different things to different people. In most cases in America, our poverty level is not as severe as many other countries around the world. However, it does exist here in America as well. I also realize that we are blessed to be living here and I thank God every day for it.

Maybe I should use the word "broke" instead of poverty. But I think you know where I am coming from. I am talking about breaking the poverty barrier and becoming "financially independent". Financial independence can mean different things to various people. It can mean being "super rich" for some people. However, it can mean having a "nest egg" of money that will allow you to not live extravagantly, but within your means. Whatever the case may be, you will not be worrying about not having enough money anymore.

I am honest enough to say that part of the reason that I am building my own brand now is to become financially independent. By becoming financially independent, I will have the resources to execute my plan (helping people worldwide) on a much larger scale. Remember, making money is a bi-product of serving people. The more you serve, the more you make. Make sense? Sounds fair to me. I am also honest enough to say that I like nice things. Most people would like to have a nice home, a nice car, and some free time to spend with your loved ones, right? I am no different, however, I must say that I am not "driven" by making as much money as I can. If that were the case, I would have given up on this journey many years ago. This is why a generous portion of all of my earnings will be donated to worthy causes, starting with the sale of my first book. As I have gotten older, I found out that in my opinion, the best way to make money is to serve and help others. Trust me, you are not taking it with you when you are gone. So hopefully you will do something good with it while you are still here. Looking back in my past, I realize that all of my business ventures (mainly failures, with some successes) were business models that made people's lives better in some way. What can I say, I am truly a "Compassionate Capitalist".

The next barrier that I intend to break is the "Mental Illness" barrier. You may know by now, that mental illness was rampant on my mother's side of the family. Mental illness has been a "silent killer" worldwide probably since the beginning of time. It's definitely a human thing. By having a mental illness myself, I feel compelled to shine a light on this highly "stigmatized" subject. Since I have been blessed enough to be born in a time where we can receive proper treatment, I feel that I owe my mother, my family (both past, present, and future) with the intention to bring awareness to this (in some cases) deadly illness.

The last barrier that I want to discuss is the "fear" barrier. FEAR (false expectations appearing real) is the biggest thief in human history. It has doused the dreams of countless people throughout human history. We humans are not born with many fears. They are learned. Now, I am not saying that fear is not real. It is definitely real, especially if you believe it. Also, by no means am I saying that I don't have fear on a daily basis. Trust me, I do. However, over the past twenty years or so, I intentionally started to work on my fears by continuously getting out of my comfort zone. By the lack of certain achievements in my early life, I realized that by being comfortable most of the time was not good for me. So as I embark on this journey, I know that I will be "scared as h#ll" some of the time. However, with God's help, I think that we make a pretty good team. There is a great song by Kenny Loggins called "Meet Me Half Way." I feel that I have an obligation to do my best to meet God halfway. It's the least that I can do for all the blessings that he has bestowed upon me. Thanks, God. Way to go!

ME TALK (TALKING IN TONGUES)

Since this is my first book, I want my readers to understand my lingo. I am a true believer that proper communication is a major key in humans understanding each other. When certain things get "lost in translation" and basic communication is lost, things can get ugly at times. I figured that this was an important topic to mention since I will be coming at you guys from various forms of what I refer to as "talk."

During my life so far, I have had the privilege to meet an incredible assortment of various ethnic groups that were also from different socioeconomic backgrounds that had their own way of talking. As an author, I believe that it is my duty to try my best to connect with you guys in a way in which you have the best chance to understand what the h#ll I am talking about. I will be using things like "hood talk," "proper talk," "man talk," "movie talk," and "country talk" to get my point across.

I hope that I am not overanalyzing this, but I want to make sure that we are on the same page. I have given this some thought because we live in a very PC (politically correct) society and I do not want to disrespect anybody. I have no judgments against anybody and believe that we are all equal and thus should be treated that way. I have LOL (lots of love) for all people. I contemplated using words like *guys* and *gals*, but I don't want to offend the LBGT community. I don't want to use *my readers* because you are not "my" readers and I do not own you. So with that said, I decided that I will address my "fan club" (just kidding) as *you, you guys*, or (since I am originally from the country and the hood) *y'all*. So I definitely hope that "you," "you guys," and "y'all are okay with this.

STORYTELLING

Since most of our lives are made up of "short stories," I decided that the best way to communicate is to write short stories. In some of my short stories, I will be using "hood talk" from an African American perspective. What does this mean and why am I mentioning this? Because in the African American community, we use the *N* word (nigga) a lot. Even back in the day, when I was a kid (at Neanderthal High), we used that now-common word. However, back in the day, we (blacks) only used it among ourselves. We would never let any other races hear us say it. Looking back, I realize that that word should have never been used, even among us.

The *N* word is used by countless people today that are both African American and otherwise. It has become a "term of endearment" for many people in our society. I am not here to pass judgment on anyone who uses it. In America, we have "FREEDOM OF SPEECH," right? However, I personally do have a problem with the *N* word because of all the historical ugliness associated with the word. So I choose to use another word that is still an *N* word but that, hopefully, works in a way that doesn't offend some people as much. I believe that this *N* word can still have the same effectiveness as the other *N* word from a storytelling perspective. However, it's kind of softer. The *N* word that I am talking about is the word *negro*. Now, the word *negro* also has a history that comes with it. But as far as I am concerned, it was a positive stepping stone along the way to finally be called African Americans. We, as a people, went through a variety of names, some not so good, to get to where we are now. I believe it started out as *nigger, negro, colored, black*, and finally, *African American*. I could be wrong, but that's my take on it.

Since I will be using movies to give certain insights, metaphors, and analogies at times, I would like to give my first example of a movie in which my version of the *N* word was used. One of my all-time favorite movies is *Pulp Fiction*. Samuel L. Jackson used my version of the *N* word when he was talking to Marsellus Wallace on the telephone. I think he said something like "All right, negro." I think using the word *negro* instead of *nigga* was just as effective as far as being funny. Not only was it effective but it also didn't sound as offensive to me. It just seems like a softer version of the *N* word. Again, I am saying that this is just my personal opinion, and it's okay to disagree. Maybe I am too "old school" and should just relax. However, I think that the best way to communicate is to be open and honest with each other, even if we disagree. So that's all for now, *negro*.

The Story of Two Lives

As I said previously, *Black Boy from the Barrio* is going to be a series of books that will be written in a short-story form. This will give me the flexibility of being able to visit the different parts of my life without having to maintain the rigidity that an autobiography would demand. However, my stories will be organized in a way that makes sense. For instance, I am starting at the beginning of my life and will continue to move forward throughout my teen years, young adult life, middle-aged life, and my senior life.

The reason that I called this "The Story of Two Lives" is because I hope to live to be at least one hundred years old. So my focus is how the first half of my life (fifty years) will differ from the second half of my life. There has been drastic changes in the way that I am living the second half of my life, and I am not talking about age or the natural "wisdom" that most of us automatically obtain as we age. I am talking about a deliberate plan to become the best person that I can become. A plan that has taken a quarter of a century so far.

For many years in the first half of my life, I was an angry black man that hated America because I believed that living in America was the sole reason that I was struggling so much. As I got older, I discovered that America was not the reason that I was unhappy. It was me and the choices that I did or did not make in my life at the time. I still believe that there is no "equal" opportunity in America. However, I believe that there is "ample" opportunity in America. Once I discovered this and took it to heart, I believed that that was all that I needed to succeed at just about any level that I chose. I decided to become part of the solution as opposed to part of the problem.

Twenty-Five Years of Striving

I had an interesting conversation with my eighteen-year-old daughter, Anikka, whom you will come to know very well in future books. Recently, she said something very profound that really resonated with me. She mentioned to me the word *striving*. By knowing me very well and by watching my daily activities, that's the word that came to her mind. Now that I think about it, and as far as I am concerned, *striving* simply means "to fail consistently and be willing to get up and fail some more." It is known to some people as "pushing the envelope." Now, I realize that this does not sound fun to most people. In fact, it can sound downright frustrating or tiresome, and you know what? It can be. However, as I said before, I have found out in the course of my life that we grow in the "valleys" (no, not the Central Valley. Sorry, I couldn't help myself) not in the "mountains."

So with that being said (and if it's okay with you), I will be writing many stories about this important word. There are many ways that we can strive; however, the first three words that come to my mind are mind, body, and spirit. Each has its unique meaning and essence, and I will be describing how they play an important role in who I am currently and the person that I wish to become in the future. Remember when I mentioned earlier that this is not all about me? Well, I really meant it. As we get to know each other more intimately—on social media or perhaps in person—I could not be more thrilled than to hear who you are and hear your story because we all have one. The main reason that I have become a writer is to connect with you and hear your voice as well.

One of my mentors told me something over twenty years ago that still sticks with me today, and I live by his words. This was at a time when I was trying to find out what determines a leader. He told me that there are two kinds of leaders. One type of leader "includes" and the other type "excludes." I am the former to the bottom of my heart and always will be. However, there is one disclaimer. I do not promote haters, trollers, or anyone else who deliberately tries to condemn people. I have no problem in critiquing or constructive criticism from anyone. I believe that "including" people is a prerequisite to becoming a better human being. One more thing he said is that true leadership is example-based leadership. Always lead by example, not by force. In most cases, if you have to lead by force or intimidation, you are not a true leader.

Getting Ahead

As I started studying success principles many years ago, one thing that I had to learn was to stop "majoring in the minors." I asked one of my mentors one day why some people are wealthy and why most people are broke or struggling. He told me that, in most cases, wealthy people don't major in the minors. This means that successful people (financial, in this case) have learned how to "invest" their time as opposed to "spending" their time. Majoring in the minors are doing things like watching too much television, social media, and other time-wasting activities.

Since being successful was a high priority to me, I DECIDED to change my activities. I started reading books, listening to tapes (caveman days), and attending business seminars at night and on the weekends. I started listening to mentors that were willing to help me for free. I was also willing to work (on my personal growth) for free.

I must say in all honesty that I am not where I want to be yet on this incredible journey thus far, but I am well on my way. Plus, success is not a destination anyway. It's a journey! As life goes on, I promise you that I will continue to "major in the majors."

GOING PUBLIC

Over the years, I have started various businesses from scratch. I also have read many books and have attended countless seminars on business development, personal growth, and success. So most of the time, when we hear the words *going public*, we (especially in the San Francisco Bay Area) think of a start-up company that wants to grow and succeed through public revenue. However, I am talking about a different kind of "going public." I am talking about me going public. I am talking about me being vulnerable or spilling my guts through writing. For most of my life, this would have been a very hard task since I am a man, and supposedly, we are all from Mars. I must admit that I am from the town of Earlimart originally, which means that I am indeed an "Earlimartian." However, I think that the woman that wrote that book had a different idea in mind. What she meant was that, in most cases, we men don't like to wear our feelings on our sleeves. Apparently, we like to go into our proverbial "man caves" and keep quiet.

One thing that I want to say about man caves before I continue. Man caves are okay when we retreat to them all alone. However, when we have our "homeboy," "road dog," "brotha from anotha motha," "podna," or whatever you choose to call your (non-hood talk) pal, it can be a blast. And what do we men talk about while in our caves? Besides watching sports on television, drinking beer, playing darts, and shooting pool, we do what I refer to as having "man talk." And what is man talk? I will be discussing more about this important topic in some of the stories when I was a child living on an eighty-acre ranch. But for now, I will give you a small example. The best way to describe what man talk is, let's see, how do I explain this. We talk sh#t about money, sports, f#ckin, p#ssy, t#ts, and a#s!

There you have it! Also, if there are any other categories that I missed, please let me know.

As we get to know one another better, I'll give you my promise that I won't be using too much of that disgusting "Martian talk," at least not on a consistent basis. However, I will be honest and truthful about my struggles and my triumphs throughout my lifetime. We good? Cool.

A Different Kind of World

Obviously, we live in a totally different world from the one that I was accustomed to for most of my life. With the invention of the internet and social media and so forth, our privacy can sometimes be threatened. I realize the life I am living right now will be forever changed as I continue this journey. Whenever a person steps out of their comfort zone and tries something new or different, she will be met with constant criticism. On the other hand, if what she is doing is worthwhile to the public, she may also be praised.

From what I have experienced thus far in my life, I expect to get both. However, criticism and rejection are a lot harder to absorb for most humans. For example, have you ever had a bunch of "likes" on social media and get just one "dislike"? How did that make you feel? If you are like most people (including me), we tend to focus on the latter. The likes will give you a warm and fuzzy feeling. However, the dislikes will give you a cold and prickly feeling.

With the internet and social media being a "double-edged sword," we have to be aware of this remarkable (and sometimes not-so-remarkable) tool. So with that being said, I am willing to expose myself to the world if necessary because I truly believe that my cause is worth it.

DADDYISMS

I will be talking about my father a lot in some of my books because his life and what it meant for all of us kids and our mother is worth mentioning. The man we called Daddy had a unique way of explaining things. He was originally from Arkansas, and he brought a lot of that "Arkansas country boy talk" with him to California. Some of those country-boy sayings not only made a lot of sense but they would also have me in stitches. I will give you an example of one of his famous sayings so you can know what I mean. "Negro, you so broke, you can't lend a crippled crab a crutch." Need I say more?

Using Colorful Language

Since, hopefully, you are getting to know me a little better by now, there is one thing that I would like for you to know about me. I rarely use what most people would consider foul language. For instance, my eighteen-year-old daughter has NEVER heard me cuss. This comes from a guy who used to cuss so much that I would make the late great comedians Richard Pryor or Redd Foxx proud. However, as I got older and started hanging around successful business people, I realized that most of them did not use "colorful" language. This is not to say that it is wrong to use any words that you wish; I just found that it's good to know when to use them and when not to use them.

For instance, I don't use colorful language in our household. However, when I am around my brothers and some of my other male counterparts, holding our tongues is not a priority. Chalk it up to male bonding, I guess. That's it, *male bonding*. Has a good ring to it, right? Let's stick with that because that sounds like a good enough of an excuse to cuss as far as I am concerned.

Finally, I would like to mention that I will be using signs like "###" in all my cuss words. Now, why would I do that? I am not sure, but it somehow makes me feel better when I am not spelling out the whole f#cking word, that's why!

Twenty-Five Years in the Making

I don't know about you, but I kind of like this "getting to know each other" stuff. To me, writing is a form of freedom in which I can express myself in certain ways in which I cannot by speaking. Have you ever spoken to a friend, boss, client or anyone else, and when the conversation was over and you both parted ways, all the important stuff that you wanted to say immediately came to your mind? Can be frustrating sometimes, right?

Now let's be clear, I am not advocating for us humans to stop talking to each other. In fact, I am all for us spending more quality time talking and communicating with each other person to person. I think that it's a lost art, especially with social media being a big part of our lives today. What I am trying to say is that if we become aware of what we are doing, then we can find a happy medium in both forms of communication. I will explain what has helped me in these opening words of this book. Someone might ask, "Then what about texting? That is a form of writing, isn't it?" As far as I am concerned, texting is a wonderful way to communicate and one that I use every day. However, I think when we text, we don't have the same timeframe and patience that writing requires, which results in us not taking the proper time to think more in-depth because we are in "replying mode." Make sense? I hope so.

I titled the above "Twenty-Five Years in the Making" because it took me roughly a quarter of a century of concerted effort just to get here. What I mean by *here* is having the knowledge, experience, motivation, and inspiration to write these words. Although this is a lifetime journey of continuous growth, I now have some clarity of how I would like to live the second half of my life. Somehow, God blessed me with the wonderful gift of ambition, patience, and a "never give up" attitude. This gift has taken me not only to various physical places on this earth but has also taken me to places in my mind that many of us would not like to visit. Discovering who you are and what your purpose is in this life is hard work, and failure is far from being fun. But I must say that once you discover your lot in life, although it will still be challenging, it will be one of the most exhilarating times a person can ever experience. I was once told by one of my mentors that once you find your passion in life, you will never work another day in your life. It will truly be a labor of love.

I will be writing fascinating stories in future chapters about my struggles both past and present. But for now, I just want my readers to get a glimpse of who I am. In most cases, I believe that as humans, our current lives are the result of prior decisions that we made or did not make. Of course there are exceptions, and I want to make sure that you don't misunderstand me. There are many exceptions to this rule, especially throughout the world in which we currently reside. However, in the Western world, especially America, most of us have the freedom to choose the direction of our lives.

In the last twenty-five years, I have made some decisions that have been critical to the way I think and the way I view things. At certain times, I didn't know if it was the right decision or not. Sometimes the decisions were the wrong ones and would set me back, so I thought. Even when the decisions were poor, I always looked at them optimistically, which meant that there was always serendipity or a silver lining involved. An example of some of my good decisions included reading on a consistent basis, getting out of my comfort zone by communicating with people regularly, exercising at least five days a week, being conscious of my diet, and most importantly, getting closer to God. I did all this while working as a house painter.

It's funny to me when people complain to me and tell me that they want to change their circumstances. Then the next words out of their mouths are "I would if I had the time." The "not having time" excuse is one of the biggest thieves that humankind has ever faced. If you truly want to change your life, don't allow this thief to slither into your mind and surround its slimy tentacles around your brain.

TO DIE FOR

I want to spend a little time about a very touchy subject, especially for us "seniors." I am still trying to wrap my head around saying that word, especially when it pertains to me. Come to think of it, I was a senior once in my life before. It was right after I was a freshman, sophomore, and a junior. Okay, I know it's not the same. However, I must admit that it doesn't bother me as much as it used to, especially when there are certain benefits that come with getting older, like senior discounts!

One of the main reasons that I became an author and a life coach was to have a positive impact on humankind. I have gone through twenty-five years of drastic changes just to get the opportunity to write these words of inspiration, motivation, and hope. Looking back, and even with the constant turmoil of failure, I would not change a thing. Why? Because I was not failing at all. In fact, I was succeeding the whole time. Deep down, I knew this in my heart, but when you are in, say, year sixteen of various business endeavors and you are still on that proverbial roller coaster, doubt sets in a little. In those challenging times, I would have to really concentrate on *why* I was doing what I was doing.

I knew that my ultimate mission in life was much bigger than me and that someday it would all start to make sense. I am happy to say that that day has arrived. Why did it take so long? My profound answer? I have no idea. I joke around and tell people that God had Moses out in the desert for forty years, so for me, twenty-five years is a cakewalk, right? (A true optimist at it again, I guess). I found out a long time ago that there is no rhyme or reason for what any given person has to go through to achieve their dreams. Everyone's path is different, so we must continue on our path or quit entirely. We cannot pay the price for other people's success, only our own. Trust me, I have seen many people succeed at high levels before me. When that happens, I can do one of two things. I can mope around and play the "poor victim" role, or I can get even more determined to achieve my own successes. Fortunately, I have chosen the latter many times during my journey. But unfortunately, I have seen countless people give up much too soon. It's kind of sad because their true potential was never realized.

This journey that I have chosen is so important to me that it is worth *dying* for. I realize that most people can't wrap their heads around that statement, and hopefully, I won't die along the way. Maybe I am just a different kind of "cat," but the older I get, the more it makes sense to me to do something significant with our lives because, let's face it, time is winding down. I know this kind of talk is making a lot of people squirm in their seats. However, if just a few people can find motivation in these words and act upon them, then I have done my job.

For the life of me, when I was younger, I couldn't understand why someone would risk their life to do certain things. People who were in law enforcement, firefighting, and the military (just to name a few) seemed silly to be involved in such dangerous professions. I also looked at risk-takers—like skydivers, rock climbers, and daredevils—as being foolish with their lives. You know what I have found out though? Some things are WORTH DYING FOR!

For some people in the military, law enforcement, and fire-fighting, etc., their cause outweighs the risk. These are some of the true heroes of our society. As for the risk-takers, like skydivers, rock climbers, and daredevils, most of them abide by a quote that I once heard many years ago: "Life is a daring adventure or nothing at all." Way to go, y'all! Keep up the good work!

Finally, I was watching television recently, and they had a segment which featured a young vibrant woman who was the world-record holder for the fastest car ever driven by a female. Unfortunately, she tragically died when her jet car lost control. The first thing that came to my mind was *What a shame.* How could a young beautiful woman risk her life doing something like that? Then I realized that if she wasn't doing what she obviously loved to do and had a passion for, then why live at all? I don't judge anyone for the way they choose to live; however, I believe that as humans, our comfort zones can sometimes be our "danger zones." Try stepping out and see how far you can go. You might be surprised. As Red quoted in the movie *The Shawshank Redemption*, "Get busy living or get busy dying." You're god d#mned right!

FATHER WHO?

By the time volume one of *Black Boy from the Barrio* is released (and through the grace of God), I will be fifty-nine years old. Funny thing about age, it seems like we have two birthdays per year after we reach the age of fifty. Feel me? (Sorry, just an OG trying to sound cool). I remember my parents always telling us kids that life is short. Of course it went in one ear and out the other, right? When we are young, many of us think that we will always be young and live forever, especially an optimist like myself. However, as the days went by, Father Time started to show up. Being an athlete, he started to invade my body, not allowing me to jump as high and run as fast as I once could. Then, at the tender age of thirty-two, he really showed his a#s as I sustained my first and only major injury. I will be telling many fascinating stories of playing basketball in upcoming books; however, I will share one story with you because it pertains to aging.

In the fall of 1992, I was playing basketball at Live Oak Park in North Berkeley. Now, Live Oak Park isn't just an ordinary park. It has both a famous and an infamous history. It's famous because the who's who of the basketball community would go there to compete and show off their skills. For decades, great players like Phil Cheneir, Al Attles, Kevin Johnson, and a long list of other players both college and pro would congregate there. It was infamous because if you didn't have game, you could get your "feelings hurt, money took, and maybe get your name on the undertaker's book."

When I started playing at Live Oak in the mid-eighties, three-on-three was the game. Not only was it a very physical game, sh#t talking was rampant. By this time in my life, I had developed a dangerous jumper. I still had some good moves to the basket and a nice little hook shot, but my jump shot was money. In fact, I was later nicknamed Cash Money from bustin' on negroes all day long. More on that later.

About three weeks before that fateful day at Live Oak Park, I was playing at Cal Berkeley's RSF (recreational sports facility). For some reason, my left Achilles tendon was a little sore. It was getting sore off and on for about a month before I played that day at Cal. Anyway, while grabbing a rebound and starting a fast break, I felt a pull on my left Achilles. I immediately limped off the court and sat down. I realized that I had probably stretched it or possibly even torn it slightly. For the next three weeks, I didn't play any basketball at all (which was very hard for me) because I spent time icing it down every day to reduce the swelling. After about a week, it started to feel better and the swelling disappeared entirely. I still waited another two weeks just to make sure it was completely healed. And it was, or so I thought.

After three weeks of taking it easy and rehabbing, I felt that I could play again. Since it was a Saturday morning, I decided to go to Live Oak and play. The three-on-three Saturday crowd would show up about 10:00 a.m. By the time I got there, they were going at it hard. I called for the next game, but I was "two down," which meant that there were two games before mine. Live Oak has a small bleacher section where everybody sat down awaiting their turn to play. I made sure that I picked two "well-seasoned" Live Oak players to join me because if you pick some "scrubs," you were sure to lose and you might as well go home because you would have to wait at the end of the line, which meant that you might be "five down."

I picked two guys that I knew were good for my team. One of the guys named was Vass, who didn't have a whole lot of raw basketball skills, but he was known as Mr. Hustle. Vass was about five feet, ten inches tall and stocky built. He was "high yella" with green eyes. Vass was very mild tempered (similar to me) and wouldn't talk too much while playing. The other guy I picked was named Poncho. Now, Poncho was different from Vass and I in that he loved to talk sh#t while he was playing. Poncho was about six feet tall, skinny, and muscular. He had a nice inside game in which he would post people up and back his way in toward the basket and score short jump shots or layups. He constantly talked as he played (Draymond Green would be proud) and would unnerve his opponents and take them out of their game. It was a great strategy. I intentionally picked these two guys because as a threesome, we had all we needed to rule the court for a while. We had Mr. Hustle (Vass), Cash Money (Me), and the Intimidator (Poncho).

After waiting about forty-five minutes, we were up next. During that time, I did some stretching, shooting, and some light running on the adjacent courts, which were available for warming up. When our game was about to start, I couldn't even remember which foot I had previously hurt, so I knew that I was ready to play again. I have had countless days at Live Oak Park in which I would "shoot the lights out." This happened to be one of those days. The team that got to twenty-four (twelve shots) points first was the winner. All I can say about my shooting on that day was that it was raining on a clear day, if you know what I mean. I remember scoring ten out of the twelve baskets that we needed to win. Out of those ten baskets that I made, nine were consecutive. After that first game, I was truly a man on fire.

As the second game started, Vass and Poncho knew that I was in a zone. They kept feeding me the ball, and I kept on "eating." Midway through the second game, I was shooting 100 percent. I had made my first six shots. I was in heaven as I could hear the "oohs" and "aahs" from the fellas sitting on the bench. Cash Money definitely had money in the bank on that day, y'all. Then, like a thief in the night, everything immediately changed.

Poncho, who was inbounding the ball, passed it to me on the wing. Vass set a good screen on my man, which gave me just enough time to catch the ball (without dribbling) and take the shot. As I took the jump shot from near the top of the circle, everything seemed fine on the way up. However, on the way down, I (and the other guys as well) heard a loud pop. I immediately felt my lower leg buckle. I looked back quickly because I thought someone had kicked me. Once I looked back and saw that nobody was there, I knew what had happened.

In the prior weeks leading up to that day, I had talked to other people who had ruptured their Achilles tendon. They told me that they, too, had thought someone had kicked them as well. A very interesting thing happened in that moment when I was grabbing my ankle that I will never forget. Once I grabbed my ankle, the first thing that I did was look up at the ball that I had released previously. With a high arch and a perfect backspin, the ball gently swished through the net. Too bad Steph Curry and Klay Thompson were not around during that time. They would have been proud. Although I had surgery and I was out of commission for ten months, Cash Money was a man on fire on that day. I guess all that I can say after that day was "Hello, Father Time."

Poquito Español

By growing up in the Central Valley town of Earlimart, I was exposed to the Mexican culture. Looking back now, I realize that my family and I were truly blessed to be a part of a culture that has so many wonderful people and that is so rich in tradition. I still have countless people that I consider friends and that are my Latino "brothers and sisters."

When we are young, most of us humans do not appreciate or are not even aware of our surroundings, so we mostly just take things for granted. One of the things that I cherish most from growing up in Earlimart is the broken Spanish language that I learned. I believe that every race has ghetto or hood talk. Not only did I learn hood talk in the black community but I also learned hood talk in the Mexican community. Of course this means that I know just about all the cuss words. Even though I have been far removed from that Latino community, I could still cuss yo a#s out in Spanish, and don't forget that, c#bron! I am definitely proud to be a black boy from the barrio.

No Mo "Hatrackin"

I know what you are thinking! You are thinking, *What the h#ll is hatrackin?* *Hatrackin* is one of the many words that I made up in my life that stemmed from the original word. Let me explain. My mother (aka Mama) used to always say to me that I should use my head for more than just a hat rack. She would usually say this to me when I was doing something silly or what she considered, (um, how should I say this) stupid! When you think about it, I guess it kind of makes sense. The human cranium is an ideal place for a hat. But I think that Mama was trying to get me to focus on the amazing three-pound pound organ (mainly made up of grey matter) that was in between my ears. "Ah, now I get it." (Sorry, it takes me a while sometimes).

During the first half of my life, I did a lot of hatrackin, and I paid a big price for it. I will give you many examples of this destructive habit in future chapters. I believe when we are young, it's okay to do a lot of hatrackin. It's a part of our natural growth process and is an important part of becoming a well-adjusted adult. However, when we get older, we can't afford to make the same mistakes as we did when we were kids. There are consequences—be it love, finances, and many other important facets of our lives that are at risk. So as I got older, I started to realize what Mama meant when she said, "No mo hatrackin." Thanks again, Mama. Way to go!

MY LIFE CURRENTLY

I consider myself to be living a very blessed life right now. Not to say that I haven't always had a good life. I definitely have, and I thank God every day for it. However, my intent is not only to have a good life but to also have a great life. To have a great life, as far as I am concerned, you must have certain things in place. Now, what I am about to say is just my opinion. However, from my experience with all the successful people that I have had the privilege to meet, the overwhelming majority of them were "wealthy." Now, when I mention the word *wealth* or *wealthy*, I am not just talking about material wealth. The people that I have met in my lifetime that I consider wealthy had wealth in many areas of their lives. For example, having wealth of character. Wealth of character is one of the virtues that they had and is something that I practice daily. They taught me five key principles that I believe are critical to having a fulfilled life. I live by and practice these principles on a consistent basis, and so can you. I keep them in a specific chronological order:

1. A spiritual connection to the higher power (God, universe, meditation, etc.)
2. A strong bond with family and friends
3. A good exercise and eating program that will hopefully keep our bodies healthy
4. A good financial plan that will allow us to be financially independent
5. A well-thought-out plan to have some "good old fun" (such as vacations)

I truly believe if you keep these five principles in order and practice them on a consistent basis, you will live a very fulfilled life that can possibly have a positive impact on others as well.

I currently live in Berkeley, California, with my wife, Kim, of forty years (twenty-seven married) and my eighteen-year-old daughter, Anikka. Kim and Anikka are MY gals, and I love them both with all my heart. I have been a part-time driver for Lyft for the last three-plus years. I have met countless people on my Lyft rides, many of which will be reading my series of upcoming books. Way to go, Lyft!

A DAY IN THE LIFE

I decided to give you an example of my daily activities so you can kind of know how I live on a daily basis right now. Again, I think that proper communication and being as transparent as possible is the key to a good and healthy relationship. I am also doing this because I realize that although I am not different or any better than anyone else, I do things differently than most people. I am a person who is driven. So knowing what you now know, whenever I am writing something, hopefully you will understand where I am coming from. Makes sense?

A typical day for me goes something like this. I wake up at 4:00 a.m. without an alarm clock. I have a prayer session, thanking God and Jesus Christ for allowing me to live another day on this earth. After that, I feed Carly, our cat, who is meowing for her morning meal. I then sit on my chair and have a thirty-minute meditation session from the Calm app. After that, I eat a banana and put my workout clothes on. I leave the house at around 5:15 a.m., headed to the local 24 Hour Fitness. I have an intense forty-five-minute circuit training session. Then I head back home, take a shower, eat a bowl of granola, pack a healthy lunch, and head for San Francisco.

I drive for Lyft for about five hours, getting back home around 1:00 p.m. I have another thirty-minute session of meditation, read at least ten pages from one of three books that I am currently reading, send and check my emails, and write until 5:00 p.m. After that, I eat a healthy dinner and have some me time (usually watching movies) until around 7:00 p.m. I spend a little family time for the rest of the evening, which means talking with my wife and daughter. At 7:30 p.m., I start unwinding for bedtime. During this thirty-minute time frame, I write in my gratitude journal, read a few passages from the

Bible, then say my nightly prayers. At 8:00 p.m., wheels down and lights out! Next day, same thing again.

Although I have a very strict schedule, I am also very flexible, meaning that I spend a lot of quality time having fun with my friends and family as well. This balance did not come easy and is still not easy. However, I think living in this particular manner is essential for my growth and will be an important part in helping me become the person that I was truly intended to be and to hopefully inspire countless others to be all that they can be as well.

Hey Y'all

Since we are REALLY starting to know each other a little better now, I would like to talk about a very important subject that is dear to my heart.

My Mental Illness

This is one of the most important topics that I will be writing about. I will be explaining how GAD (generalized anxiety disorder) is a part of this second half of my life. I will go into specific detail explaining how it effects my life and how I manage to keep the symptoms under control. I found that being open and honest about my condition is the best way to heal not only for myself but for countless others as well. I have become a mental health advocate, which means that I have a life-long commitment to helping others face various mental illnesses as well. I will be writing many chapters on this world-wide epidemic.

However, let me share my story first. I believe that being open and honest is truly the best policy, even when it can sometimes be difficult. So here goes. FYI…the following few pages were written in the fall of 2018. I think giving you guys the uncut version of what I was thinking at that time is the best way to express how I was feeling during the fall of 2018.

COMING OUT OF A DIFFERENT CLOSET (AS AN AFRICAN AMERICAN MALE)

When the phrase "coming out of the closet" is expressed by someone, it usually means that someone in the gay, lesbian, LGBT, etc. community is making a statement about coming out of hiding in regard to their sexuality or gender. I would like to talk about another topic that millions of people suffer through alone, and that is mental illness.

This is one of the extremely difficult subjects that I will be writing about within my writing experience. But I believe it is one of the most important ones. I have two choices: (1) I can be silent about my mental illness and try to live a quiet life, or (2) I can be a shining light to perhaps help others. I choose the latter.

I want to talk openly about mental illness and how it impacts my life currently. I would really like to reach out to as many people as I can about this common but difficult subject, especially men. There is still a stigma attached to mental illness in our society, and I want to be an advocate and talk about our struggles; hopefully, this will bring more awareness to the millions of sufferers who think that they are somehow different and that they have to fight this illness alone or try to alleviate their symptoms through an unprescribed controlled substance. From what I experienced so far in the last year, I realize that mental illness isolates us and puts us in a box in which depression can occur. I want to be a positive voice to the countless people who suffer from serious mental illnesses like schizophrenia, which my mother has been battling for most of her life. I want to bring an understanding to my family about our family's history of mental illness, which was very prevalent within my mother's family tree, and how it may affect future generations.

I realize that there are many forms of mental illnesses, some more serious than others, but I will be focusing on anxiety—and depression-based mental illnesses, which are the most common in the world today and the ones that I am currently battling. I am by no means saying that I am a psychologist, psychiatrist, or a therapist. However, I must say within the last year of holistic treatment, therapy sessions, antidepressants, and in-depth research, I have one thing that will hopefully get people's attention, and that is my personal experience. One of the biggest conversations with my Lyft passengers the past few months have been about anxiety and depression. Once our conversation starts and they ask me about my life, I tell them that I am writing memoirs about my life. After giving them a brief history of my past life, I make sure to include what's going on in my current life.

The first thing that I mention is my GAD (generalized anxiety disorder). The reason that I do this is that I am a true advocate of mental illnesses and also know that there is a good chance that my passenger might be experiencing some kind of symptoms, especially women. I know this because of the extensive research that I've done, knowing that anxiety and depression occurs in more women than men. I don't know why this is supposedly true, but most experts agree on this. Most of my conversations on Lyft rides have been with women. When I mention my mental illness to both male and female passengers, the female passengers are overwhelmingly more open to talking about it than their male counterparts. Of course I know why this is. Apparently, the stigma of mental illness runs a lot deeper in men than it does in women. Most men are taught from an early age to not show signs of weakness. Even though I believe expressing ourselves is therapeutic, most men don't want to discuss this topic.

ANXIETY AND DEPRESSION (YOU DO YOU)

These forms of mental illnesses are treatable; however, everyone is different, meaning that each individual who seeks treatment must find out what works best for them. There are different remedies such as holistic options, therapy, and antidepressants. You might need one or two of these options or a combination of all three or maybe none at all. Personally, I have had to use three of these options at one time or another, but you may not. Again, everyone is different, so I hope that you find out what works best for you.

But there is hope. I have the symptoms of GAD (generalized anxiety disorder) The classic symptoms are excessive worrying, restlessness, irritability, loss of appetite, and insomnia. Depression is commonly linked with this disorder as well, in which I, also, have occasionally experienced. Other mental illnesses such as OCD, PTSD, panic disorder, and socialized anxiety disorder are other mental disorders that are very common in our society today and are similar to GAD in some ways.

WHAT IS HAPPENING TO ME? (I FEEL DIFFERENT)

To explain what having a mental illness is like is a little difficult, but I will try my best to explain. I remember when I was younger and still living at home with my parents in the barrio and my mother (who is schizophrenic) would walk the streets in Earlimart and would bring piles of garbage into the front yard of our house. Of course this would infuriate my father to no end. He just could not understand what would compel a person to do this. I will never forget what he said one day to me as my mother approached the house with yet another shopping cart of junk.

He said, "Son, do you think your mother knows right from wrong or is she just doing this to make me mad"?

I told him that I was not sure, knowing that picking sides among my parents' problems and arguments was something that I (and most other kids in this world) was not going to do. It was a no-win situation. The reason that I am saying this is because now that I have GAD, I can tell that I don't have schizophrenia. Through my research so far and living with this illness for over a year now, I can honestly say that I have never acted in a way that would suggest that I am mentally unstable.

MY CHALLENGING "EPISODE"

I started experiencing symptoms such as anxiety and insomnia in the summer of 2017. It's kind of hard to explain, but I felt a little off. It's kind of like hitting a wall of some kind. My focus and concentration declined in some areas of my life. I also lost interest in certain activities, like watching sports and reading the newspaper. I would have different mood swings that I had never experienced before in my life. I have always been a happy-go-lucky kind of a guy with a very positive and optimistic look on life. Fortunately, that part of me never changed even on the most challenging days. I am currently taking antidepressants and have had six months of therapy sessions. This has not been easy for me because I don't even like taking aspirin for an occasional headache. So it's been a very humbling and surreal experience and reminds me that our health can change in an instant and to not take things for granted.

When these symptoms started, I was very happy and satisfied with my life and the direction it was headed. It must be biological or hereditary because everything seemed fine to me. I had just changed to a better job, and I was working on some exciting business projects. I had just signed up for a course to become a certified life coach in early September of 2017, which I completed. Becoming a life coach would be a way for me to help people in some of the areas that I was experienced in. Human relations, goal setting, time management, dream-building, and discipline are some of my strong points. But mostly, I have a love for people and inspiring them to be all they can be and to reach their highest potential. At the same time, I have always felt that I should reach my highest potential as well.

LIKE A TON OF BRICKS

For some reason, I started feeling stressed out one day, and when the stress didn't go away in a day or two like it usually did, I became concerned. I started to get stressed out about being stressed out, if that makes any sense. Soon after that, the insomnia came along and, at times, has been chronic and very severe. There have been times where I wouldn't sleep for two to three days straight and would have to miss work because I was too zombie-like to go. After nine months of very tough symptoms from my mental illness without medication, I decided to call my primary care physician (PCP) and discuss some alternatives. I had already been given a thorough examination by him nine months before, and he had determined that I was totally healthy. He suggested that I should try taking an antidepressant to help with my anxiety.

After taking twenty-five milligrams of an antidepressant for about six weeks, I was still having trouble with sleeping. The toughest times were when I wouldn't sleep all night and couldn't go to work. I realized the severity of my illness when I would miss at least three days of work per week. There were countless days in which I would tell Kim that I was not able to get up and go to work. I went to work plenty of days on three hours or less of sleep. Some days I would go without any sleep at all if it was just one night. Of course, I wouldn't drive if I was up for two or three days in a row. That would be risking my life and the passengers' lives that were riding with me.

One of the most debilitating things about chronic and severe insomnia after lying awake all night without any sleep is not being able to sleep in the daytime as well. So not only did I not go to work but I would also stay in bed until around 10:00 a.m. without any sleep. I can't count the days that I watched my seventeen-year-old daughter (Anikka) put her makeup on in our bedroom before going to school. I realized that I had to get up at some point. I couldn't just lie there in a fetal position all day long. I would finally get up and eat a bowl of granola and head to the gym for my daily workout. I knew that a good workout would make me feel somewhat human again. My workout sessions and my daily meditation practice became two of the most important activities through this difficult time. I never missed a workout or meditation session even after having been up for several days at a time. There were many "zombie" days, but I never missed a single session of these very important practices because I knew that they were critical in the healing process of mental illnesses.

CAN I JUST BE A CAT?

When we humans are experiencing STORMS in our lives, it's not unusual to compare ourselves to others. Somehow, we think other people's lives are perfect, so we are prone to comparing our lives to the lives of people that are considered perfect from our perspective. Their images and supposedly great lifestyles are everywhere. From television, magazines, the media, and other various forms of the "Madison Avenue" lifestyle, we can feel sad or even depressed at times.

Now, I am by no means knocking celebrities or people who are in what we consider "high places." Most of those people have worked their tails off to get to where they are now, and they should live their lives to the fullest. My point is that we (myself included) COMPARE ourselves to these people at times, and it's not fair to us. It's a losing proposition. Here's why. Whenever we compare ourselves to others, we always compare their STRENGTHS to our WEAKNESSES. It's a game that we will never win.

Now, with all that said, I will talk about why I thought being a cat might not be so bad. Of course I'm kidding, but sometimes our struggles in life gives us a different perspective. As I was saying earlier, comparison is not a good thing, right? In the first few months of 2018, from January to May, I experienced the worst time of my battle with insomnia. These were the times when it was chronic and severe, which also made my anxiety go through the roof. Now, what does this have to do with a cat? Anyway, we have a cat named Carly, and I am her primary caretaker. I feed her, clean out her litter box every day, scratch her back, give her special treats, and let her in and out of the house constantly. In other words, she is living like a queen. Not bad for an alley cat that was adopted from a shelter.

On some of my worst nights and days of not sleeping, she would be curled up in a ball next to the warm heater or be lying in our bed next to me asleep when I was up for two days straight. After thinking about her cushy lifestyle and what I was going through at the time, I couldn't help but think, *I wouldn't mind being a cat—more specifically Carly—right now.* Then I remembered one of my golden rules. It's not good to compare, even if it's Queen Carly the cat.

GRATITUDE THROUGH MEDITATION AND MINDFULNESS

Meditation is a holistic activity that I practice on a daily basis. After my morning prayer, I meditate every morning before heading off to work out. I also have an afternoon meditation session when I get home from work. As I stated earlier, I use a meditation app called Calm. I highly recommend it for anyone whether you have a mental illness or not. Tamara Levitt (founder and CEO of Calm) does an excellent job of giving mostly "guided meditations." Her vast knowledge of various meditation practices can be essential to a person looking to find peace in the busy world that we live in. She also teaches mindfulness, which is a practice that teaches us to be mindful (aware) of ourselves and our surroundings without judgment. I realize that this may sound odd to some people, but placing judgments on everything (mainly ourselves) can be harmful at times. Our inner critic can sometimes be ruthless.

Meditation and mindfulness creates space in the mind. The goal is to retrain our mind in a way that creates inner peace and less stress and anxiety. It's kind of like a workout for the brain. The mind and the body are connected, so in my opinion, I believe as humans that we should have a consistent exercise program for both of these important areas in order to live happier lives. When I first heard about mediation, I thought that I would have to become a Buddhist and get all "zinned" out and chant for hours with a group of people. There is nothing wrong with that of course, if you prefer to practice in that way. However, I wanted it to be more personal and have more time flexibility since my work schedule is kind of rigid. Thank goodness for modern technology in which I can get guided meditations through an app. As far as I am concerned, some of the guided meditations that I listen to are as effective as some of the one-on-one therapy sessions that I was attending at a certain time during this process. I meditate on things like self-acceptance, gratitude, being present, loving kindness, and a plethora of other subjects.

Like my daily workout sessions, I have not missed a single prayer and meditation session. I realized many years ago through my business training, that there is a formula to success. To be successful at anything, it takes persistent and consistent activity over a certain time period to get positive results. This rule definitely applies to my workout and meditation sessions as well. These are lifetime projects for me.

YOU ARE NOT ALONE

As I started learning more about mental illnesses in general and people that had similar symptoms in which I was experiencing, I realized that I would have to come to grips with the fact that I was one of the tens of millions of people worldwide who was struggling with this illness. Initially, I did not want to accept the fact that I would be the only family member, besides my mother, that might be mentally ill. But the persistent insomnia, lack of appetite, and other symptoms made it very plain to me that I might have some kind of mental illness.

After countless hours of research and reading many blogs and forums, I realized that everyone is different in their body chemistry, so you must find out what remedies to use for yourself. Although some of the blogs and articles on the internet were helpful, some of them would scare the living daylights out of me and would make my anxiety worse. There were many warnings that people were giving about certain medications that they were taking that made their symptoms worse or did not work at all. I wasn't sure if I needed medication or not. I was meditating and exercising daily for nine months. I was also seeing a therapist on a weekly basis. My insomnia was persistent, but I was still able to function at some capacity.

I had tried over-the-counter sleeping aids like Melatonin and a wide array of different sleeping aids, including a prescribed dose of Trazodone (which is often used for insomnia) from my doctor. The Trazodone helped me sleep better at times when I just started taking it. However, as the months went by, it lost its effectiveness. I even tried CBD oil, which is a marijuana extract and works well for some people. I also had acupuncture sessions for a brief period as well. EFT (emotional freedom technique) is another form of a holistic way to treat symptoms of mental illnesses as well as many other ailments and problems concerning humans. EFT or "tapping" is well-received by many well-known specialists. I would recommend it for anyone. You can google Nick Ortner for more information.

After all these experimental remedies, my insomnia persisted, which meant my anxiety was still a problem as well. Most of my anxiety came from the thought that I might not sleep the next night, so the thought of not sleeping became my biggest problem. Even after a good night's rest, I would start thinking about how I might not sleep the next night. To all of you reading this that suffer from insomnia, you know what I am talking about, right? It can be debilitating. I needed help from somewhere or anywhere that could help me sleep. There were a couple of occasions, after being awake for two days straight, that I was ready to go to the emergency psych ward for help. I mentioned this to Kim, and she asked if I was 51/50, meaning was I mental unstable? I told her no and that my brain was sharp as a tack. I just couldn't fall asleep.

I had tried all the recommended remedies such as drinking warm milk before bedtime, shutting off my iPhone an hour before, reading a book if I couldn't fall asleep, or moving to a different room. None of these worked for me. My anxiety would continue to soar as the night went on. I could tell by my rapid heartbeat while lying awake in bed. At that time, I knew that it was going to be a long night. I had my share of "night fights," which were mental battles within my mind, while trying to fall asleep. Once I got to the point where I was trying to fall asleep, I knew that it was all over. I knew that it was going to be another long night. I came up with a definition for insomnia. Having insomnia is "watching and waiting" for yourself to fall asleep. By doing this, of course, falling asleep is impossible. During this difficult time of sleeplessness, I listened to Tamara Levitt's program on understanding insomnia. As tough as this process was, I continuously listened to her guided meditations on anxiety and how it affects our sleep pattern. It was huge in helping me not only to understand how sleep works but also helping me get some good nights of rest and sleep during that tumultuous time.

TAKING THE PLUNGE (CAN ANTIDEPRESSANTS BE THE ANSWER?)

One of the many things that I learned while researching these types of mental illnesses were that so many people were using antidepressants to help alleviate their symptoms. Some people praised them, and other people said that they didn't have any effect on them or made their symptoms worse. So I had a decision to make. At that particular time, I heard through the grapevine that one of my family members was experiencing similar symptoms to mine. This was the first time that I realized what the many people on the internet along with my constant research was proving: that mental illness (anxiety and depression) is very common throughout the world. My family member had recently started taking antidepressants that were prescribed by his PCP (primary care physician). He was also seeing his PCP on a weekly basis for therapy sessions. This was a shock to me because he would be one of the last people that I would think of who might have a problem with anxiety or depression because of his carefree and happy disposition.

I called him one day, and we spoke openly about our mental illnesses and how the stigma is still attached to it, especially with men. He has socialized anxiety disorder, which means he gets very uncomfortable being around crowds of people. Now I understand why he would not show up for many family events. I, as well as other family members, thought that he was being insensitive and was being a flake. After my insomnia problems were revealed to my sister-in-law by my wife, Kim, she opened up by telling Kim that her husband was having similar problems and that he was seeing a therapist. Kim recommended that I call him to see what was going on. So I did.

After not reaching him directly by phone, I left a voicemail for him. He called me back later that day. He told me that he was experiencing extreme anxiety while at work. He is a self-employed contractor that has been in business for many years. We had worked on projects from time to time when I was in the house painting business. He told me that his anxiety was so intense that he could not manage a building project. His employees asked him if he was okay, and he told them, "No, I am not okay." He was also experiencing insomnia, which I stated earlier is a common side effect of anxiety and depression.

By the time that I had reached out to him, he told me that he was doing much better. Apparently, he has been dealing with anxiety and depression for many years without knowing what it really was. He thought that he was naturally kind of anxious and never thought much about it. He started having sleeping problems in high school and just decided that he was also just a bad sleeper. Chances are that he had the anxiety disorder when he was a teenager and never got treatment because he did not realize that there was a problem. He had been sleeping only half the night for decades and had learned to accept it. I guess that he realized that it was his "own reality" and did not think much about it. Most of his nights, from about 1:00 a.m. until about 5:00 a.m., he would be reading books. After that, he would get ready for work. He was fifty-eight years old when his anxiety reached a boiling point. I think that stress and anxiety builds up over time and, if not properly treated, can have serious effects on one's mental and physical health.

OPENING UP (IT'S A GOOD THING)

My brother-in-law told me that his wife suggested that he visit his PCP. Apparently, some primary care physicians will recommend and prescribe antidepressants and counseling to their patients. He told me that his wife had mentioned this a few times before, but of course, like most men, he wouldn't consider seeing a "shrink" because that would mean that he was weak in some kind of way. What I have learned so far in my journey with mental illness is that it will break you at some point. No person can live with the symptoms of anxiety and depression for too long. They are simply too uncomfortable to live with.

I have a heavy heart for the people that try to relieve the symptoms with the use of alcohol or some other illegal or unprescribed drugs. Some people, mostly men, do the unimaginable by committing suicide. So as you can see, this is some very serious stuff that I am talking about here. My brother-in law finally gave in to what his wife was saying after his latest episode. She told him that he needed professional help. By the time I had called him, he was taking antidepressants and had been in therapy for several weeks with his PCP. This was good for me because I now had someone who I knew had a similar condition to mine and could offer some insight. Also, it made me feel better knowing that I was not alone in what I was going through. I guess that misery loves company, right?

My brother-in-law told me that his first therapy session was very helpful for him. All he did was talk nonstop the whole session without allowing his PCP to get a word in edgewise. Finally, at the end of the session, his PCP recommended that they meet again the following week. He also suggested that he should consider taking an antidepressant. He told me that after his first therapy session with his PCP, he felt much better just having someone to talk to that would listen. I definitely understand because, as I alluded to earlier, mental illnesses have a way of making you feel alone and isolated; so I wasn't surprised when he told me that he was a complete chatterbox for the whole session.

THEY'RE WORKING FOR ME

As we continued our conversation, my brother-in-law told me that the antidepressants along with the therapy sessions were helping him. He said that it took about five weeks for the medication to work. This is very typical when taking an SSRI (selective serotonin reuptake inhibitor). I know. I'm sounding way too technical right now, but I did my research on these drugs knowing that I might need to take them at some point. I wanted to know what I would be putting in my body and how some of the side effects would affect me.

I have learned a lot about the different drugs and what they are used for. It's kind of sobering when you read about these drugs and what they are used for. Some of them may cause suicidal thoughts, which scared me a little. I started to realize that mental illness is no joke and some of the medications used for alleviating the symptoms were serious and could cause harm or even death if used improperly. I realized that I was playing in the "big leagues" now. However, the best thing about the whole process of reaching out to my brother-in-law and learning more about these drugs was that our mental illnesses brought us closer and allowed us (two men) to speak openly about our fears. We still contact each other often, wondering how the other person is doing.

OH MY GOD, YOU TOO?

Kim has another sister that lives in Berkeley as well. She is also married, which means that I have another brother-in-law living nearby. Anyway, a few months ago, he needed to stop by to pick up something from our place. I was the only one at home at the time. He asked how I was doing, and I told him that I was having trouble with insomnia. I invited him in, and we sat on the couch and started to chat. He told me that he had a mild case of OCD (obsessive-compulsive disorder) and anxiety. He took two kinds of medications (antidepressants) and attended therapy on a weekly basis. He didn't have insomnia, which is a blessing for him, believe me.

Our simple chat turned into a full-blown conversation about mental illnesses, medications, and side effects. We both realized that we were both in the same boat and that we had something more in common than just being in-laws. We felt a bond toward each other that has allowed us to become closer. We now text each other often to see how everything is going. We talk to each other a lot at family gatherings now about our mental illnesses and how we are dealing with them. Talking about this openly to each other has been very therapeutic for the both of us.

HOOK ME UP, DOC

After talking with both my brothers-in-law, I decided that taking antidepressants might be a solution for me as well. I also knew that my chronic insomnia could lead to depression if not properly treated. I visited my PCP, and he told me that I was suffering from anxiety. At this time, I was in therapy and practicing holistic remedies such as a daily meditation practice and EFT (emotional freedom techniques). Although these practices helped in some ways, I still knew that I needed something more. My PCP recommended that I start taking an antidepressant called Zoloft.

Zoloft (sertraline) is used for a wide array of different mental illnesses, including anxiety and depression. So after listening to him and doing my own extensive research, I decided that I should give it a try. After taking one twenty-five milligram pill of Zoloft in the morning, I immediately got diarrhea. At this particular time during my journey, I was averaging about three to four hours of sleep per night. After taking that Zoloft pill that morning, I was awake ALL night. I was due to take my second dose that morning. I figured that I didn't need this stuff. I felt that I could sleep badly by myself. Anyway, I called my PCP, and he encouraged me to continue taking the meds. Some of them would take anywhere from four to six weeks to become effective. Side effects are common, so if I wanted to be on medication, this was the process. Kim thought that it was a good idea to get on the meds as well. She realized something needed to be done because she had a front-row seat and was witnessing my challenges firsthand.

OUT OF POCKET
(OUCH!)

When I first started experiencing symptoms of GAD in the fall of 2017, Kim and I realized that we would be visiting specialists like doctors, therapists, and perhaps psychiatrists. At the time, this didn't bother us because I had health insurance. I have had a major insurance carrier for at least twenty-five years, and we never missed a payment. I used the insurance just once when I tore my Achilles tendon when I was thirty-two years old. I honestly can't remember what my co-pay was since it was so long ago. After that incident, I never used it again. We just paid the premiums every month for years.

Once we figured out that I needed to see a primary care physician, we called the carrier to locate a doctor that was in their network. They found a local holistic doctor that was nearby. We visited the doctor and filled out all the necessary paperwork and insurance forms. My doctor gave me a quick examination and suggested that I get some blood work done with one of their local affiliates. After all the tests were taken. I was happy to see that I was totally healthy. Because I wasn't sleeping well, he prescribed me with a small dose of Trazodone, which is an antidepressant; however, if used in small dosages, it can help with insomnia, like I mentioned before. My doctor also recommended that I see a therapist on a weekly basis as well. Acupuncture was also a holistic practice that he said might work. After hearing all this, I told Kim, "Boy, I'm quite a piece of work, huh?

After the doctor's visits, lab work, acupuncture sessions, and therapy, we found out that my health insurance would not cover ANY of this. We called them and diligently went through our policy with a manager, and apparently, my issues were not covered. Of course, this was disappointing to us since we were long-time customers. However, this is an example of the broken medical system in America. I am in no way putting shade on my insurance carrier. This is the policy that I was paying for. Like many people, we didn't know what we had until we NEEDED it. We bought this policy because we could afford it. We did some research on some policies that would cover these types of problems. And of course, they were double or triple the amount that we were paying monthly for my plan. My advice to you guys is to check your coverage before you need it, especially if it is a PPO plan.

SORRY, NICKI
(REST IN PEACE,
MY DARLING ANGEL)

One of the most challenging times that I had was in the spring of 2018. At this particular time, my insomnia had gotten to the point in which it became even more chronic and severe, meaning that any partial sleepless nights became full sleepless nights. My sleep pattern was so erratic that I went a whole month sleeping every other day. I missed fifteen nights of sleep that month. It was the strangest thing. Can you imagine sleeping like a baby one night, and then being totally awake all night the next? For some reason, I could not sleep for two nights in a row. On the other hand, I would not sleep at all for two consecutive nights occasionally. My worst encounter was when I was up for three days straight. As you can imagine, this was debilitating. I had to face the truth. I was in a crisis.

During these very challenging times, the unthinkable occurred. My sister Charlotte called me from her home in Marietta, Georgia, telling me that our niece, Nicole, had passed away. Nicole was the only child of my older sister Christine. Nicole was originally from Tulare, California, which is located in the heart of the Central Valley. She was only forty years old, and she was the first of our nieces and nephews to pass away. This was a stark reminder of how precious life is and when my father would always say to us that "Death is not prejudiced." He was right.

Nicole had moved to the Los Angeles area after high school to attend Cal State Northridge. I was in contact with her periodically in the late nineties helping her out financially for school matters.

During that time, I had a business meeting in the Los Angeles area and invited her to dinner. We went to a local TGI Friday's restaurant in which I treated her to a dinner. Little did I know that would be the last time that I would see her alive. For some reason, Nicole was a loner and decided not to contact her family. She and her mother (my sister Christine) would chat periodically by phone from time to time, but that was about it. We never understood why she disowned her loved ones, but perhaps she had a compelling reason. None of us could think of a reason why she would abandon us since we had shown her nothing but love. Anyway, it was her decision to make, and although I never understood her decision, I accepted her privacy and the life in which she wanted to lead.

When Charlotte broke the news to me, I was both shocked and saddened. I won't go into any details on how she passed away because I haven't gotten permission from Nicole's mother to tell this chapter of her daughter's life. Hopefully, I will be able to expand on the story of her life someday, so she won't be forgotten.

As I was saying earlier, my insomnia, along with my anxiety were at an all-time high. The memorial services for Nicole would occur in two weeks and would be in Long Beach, California. I initially agreed that I would be attending because missing her funeral was not an option for me as far as I was concerned. I had attended the funeral of my cousin from Earlimart (Halean Cobb) about two months prior to Nicole's. At that point and time, my insomnia was not considered chronic and severe since I was sleeping at least a portion of most nights. However, on the day of Halean's funeral, I was in Visalia at my mother-in-law's house with Kim, and I was up all night. I didn't get a wink of sleep. Even though I was exhausted, I still managed to make it through the service. Attending important family events has always been something that I believe I should attend, especially funerals.

As Nicole's memorial date got closer, my insomnia got worse. Just the thought of me traveling all the way from Berkeley to Long Beach for two days and sleeping in a different bed made my anxiety worse. My insomnia went from acute, which is somewhat manageable, to chronic and severe, which means that I could be awake for several days at a time. I decided that I would see how I was sleeping the week before the memorial service before I would make my decision on whether to attend or not. Two days before the service, I had not slept at all, so I had to make the unthinkable decision of not attending our darling Nicole's memorial service. This is an example of how debilitating mental illness can be at times.

I'VE GOT SOME NEWS

As the memorial day for Nicole got closer, I knew that I would not be attending. I had talked to Charlotte about a week and a half before, explaining my mental illness situation. I felt that it would be a good time to let the family know what was going on. I chatted with Charlotte for about an hour on that day about the abrupt changes in my life. I asked her to inform the other members of our family so they would know what was going on as well. I hoped that they would understand, and they did.

A CALL FROM WANDA

After the memorial service for Nicole, I got a call from my older sister, Wanda. By not attending an important event like Nicole's memorial service, Wanda became concerned. Charlotte had informed the other siblings that I was experiencing some problems. Wanda was not sure what my problems were really about, only that I was not sleeping well. I informed Wanda that I had GAD and that insomnia was one of the symptoms. After telling her that, she opened up and told me that she had panic attacks, which is panic disorder. She explained how frightening it was for her and how she suffered an attack at work and an ambulance was called to take her to a nearby hospital. Then she mentioned something to me that surprised me. She said that she was embarrassed by the incident, having her co-workers see her hauled away in an ambulance.

After hearing her say that to me, it reminded me that most people with mental illnesses have shame about having this very common disorder. I encouraged her that there was nothing to be ashamed of. I really think that she appreciated me talking to her and relating to her since we both have similar illnesses. The conversation with Wanda is a perfect example that society at large still holds a stigma to mental illnesses. She was taking antidepressants for six years (however, not anymore) without any family members knowing about it except for perhaps our oldest sister, Netta, since she and Wanda are so close to one another. As I said earlier, mental illness and depression can isolate you and put you in a box, which can have devastating effects on people and which sometimes can lead to the unthinkable, which is suicide.

Wanda and I chatted for about an hour straight, in which I can never remember doing so in our entire lives. There is definitely a stronger bond between us now, which is great. She has called me again recently within the last month or so to see how I was doing. Again, we talked for about an hour, which made our bond even closer. Before our first chat, I thought that I was the only child among us siblings that had signs of a mental illness. Boy, was I wrong. Wanda told me that another one of my family members is taking Paxil, which is an antidepressant used for a variety of mental illnesses. This shocked me because I had always viewed this family member as unflappable and the "rock" of the family.

As you can see, we humans have our own views and opinions of how we see others. I have been working diligently not to prejudge people, especially as I've gotten older. We all have certain prejudices that we should continue to try to alleviate. It's a part of being human. Most prejudices can be overcome if your heart is in the right place, which means you are open to understanding as opposed to judgment. I have since talked to other family members and discovered that I am definitely not alone. Since I have opened up, I believe that all of us siblings (as well as other family members, such as cousins and so on) are building a closer bond to each other. My goal is to have a positive effect on future generations of my family so they won't have to go through the same stigma challenges that we and our predecessors had to face.

SIMON SAYS

In the spring of 2018, I had hit rock bottom, as far as I was concerned. For nine months, I had valiantly fought the symptoms of my GAD mainly through holistic remedies. In mid-April, after missing Nicole's funeral, I was still plagued by severe anxiety and insomnia. I remember hitting a breaking point when my PCP told me that he would only prescribe certain medications that he deemed safe for mental health issues. As I said earlier, he prescribed twenty-five mgs of Zoloft per day, in which I just started taking. He would not prescribe sleep medications like Ambien because he said that it could be habit-forming. He recommended that I see a psychiatrist because he believed that I could get the help that I needed.

During this "rock bottom" period, I could feel the clutches of depression starting to settle in on my psyche. One morning, after lying in bed and not being able to go to work, I did something that I never thought I would do in my wildest dreams. I visited the Social Security and Disability website to see what kind of payments I could receive if I continued on this path. For a dreamer and an entrepreneur at my very core, just to be researching these websites describes just how low that I had fallen. Just to be clear, I am not condemning people who need these services. There is definitely a place in our society in which these benefits help many people. However, by the grace of God, so far, I am not one of them.

I remember lying in bed on a Thursday morning in April 2018. I had been up for two days, and I was desperate. I took my PCP's advice and started to call local psychiatrists. What really concerned me was that it usually takes a while to find someone that is available. Even when you do find someone, it can take a few days or weeks before you get to see them.

While lying in bed, I started calling numerous psychiatrist's offices and leaving messages about who I was and why I was calling. After about an hour and a half of calling, I finally got out of bed and ate my morning granola. After taking a shower, I noticed that someone had called back. As I listened to the recorded voicemail, I wasn't sure if the person that called back was legitimate or not. His voice sounded, how can I say this, very "old." He got my immediate attention when he said that he had a cancellation the next day and if I could come to his office the next morning. Old or not, this was music to my ears. I promptly called him back and set the appointment.

After setting the appointment and being a little skeptical of this person, I did a background check. After I did the background check, it all started to make sense. Dr. Simon had been in practice for sixty-two years. He had various awards for his work throughout his career and had a good rating on Yelp. Yet again, I learned the valuable lesson of never judging a book (even if it's very old) by its cover.

It was a surreal and humbling experience visiting Dr. Simon. As I walked into the waiting room of Dr. Simon's office, I noticed some of the certificates that he had received showing his qualification as a psychiatrist. It suddenly dawned on me that I, Neo Wright, was visiting a psychiatrist. I have seen countless movies in which I saw people sitting on the proverbial couch. I never imagined in my wildest dreams that I would ever be on the "couch side" of a psychiatrist's office. It was very surreal and very humbling. However, it didn't take me long to stop thinking about that sh#t. This negro needed help, and I needed it now!

As I walked into Dr. Simon's office, the first thing that I noticed was that he didn't even have a couch in there. He had me sit in a very comfortable chair. So much for Hollywood and the movies. The first thing that he asked me was "Mr. Wright, you look worried."

The little voice in my head that sounds like Samuel L. Jackson sometimes said, "Hell yeah, motherf#cka. I haven't slept in d#mn near three days. What the f#ck do you expect?" Of course, I didn't say that out loud and realized that I was very blessed to be there.

Dr. Simon also had an old hound dog in his office that I am sure was older (in doggy years) than he was. What a pair! This man was not only old school, he was going medieval on my a#s (another word used in *Pulp Fiction*, remember?). Anyway, as he started to ask me questions, I immediately started to get more comfortable by the moment. It didn't take me long to realize that Dr. Simon knew his stuff. I explained my situation to him, and he told me that there were many options available (as far as prescription medications) that we could try.

Just by hearing his words of encouragement, I felt much better immediately. He recommended that I up my dosage of Zoloft from twenty-five mgs to fifty mgs. Then he said that he would write me a prescription for Valium. He explained to me that Valium was not a sleeping pill; however, it should calm my mind during bedtime. I was a little concerned because I had heard the term *Valium* before, and it was not said in a positive sense. Apparently, Valium has been used as a recreational drug for decades and has been abused by many people.

At this particular time of my mental illness venture and sleeping very little, I didn't give a fat rat's patoody (hope that's not a bad word because I didn't use ###, like I usually do) what he prescribed. As long as it was not heroin, which I knew was a bad drug, I told Dr. Simon (as we often said in the hood), "Come on wit' it."

After taking the prescribed ten mgs of Valium about thirty minutes before bedtime, I slept like a baby every night before visiting him a week later for a follow-up appointment. Through medication, meditation, exercise, and eating a healthy diet, I felt human again.

BACK ON TRACK

Since visiting Dr. Simon last year, I have been sleeping well. I will have an occasional partial night's sleep. But that's about it. I have changed psychiatrists within the last few months because, apparently, Dr. Simon WAS really old. He retired at the end of 2018. My new psychiatrist, Dr. Kumar Vedantham, is great. He recommended that I reduce my Valium intake and drop the dosage to a safer level. He said that ten mgs might not be safe in the long run. He asked if I would be open to trying another drug that is used especially for sleeping. I told him that I would.

So to update you guys on what I am taking now and how everything is going, here goes. I am happy to say that within the last year and a half, I have been sleeping well and I have been back to my usual bada#s self. I have reduced the Valium to two mgs per day with a goal of getting off it entirely in the near future. I still take fifty mgs of Zoloft, and I started taking twenty mgs of Zaleplon (sonata) for sleeping.

Finally, I must say that with all the meds and all my holistic activities that I do, I don't know exactly what is working and how it's working. All I know is that SOMETHING is working. But ultimately, I know in my heart what really is working. All I have to do is look up into the sky and say, "Thank you." Also, a shout-out to all the wonderful people in the psychiatric world who help people like me. I am forever grateful.

Lastly, I would like to thank my PCP, Dr. Anas Hana, who helped me medically and steered me in the right direction when I was in a crisis. Also, Kayo Sumisaki, who was my therapist for about six months. Her therapy sessions were just what I needed at the time. And last but certainly not least, the two psychiatrists that were critical to getting me back on track, which were Dr. Justin Simon and Dr. Kumar Vendantham. Way to go, everybody!

SHOUTING FROM A MOUNTAINTOP

As I said earlier, I will be an advocate for people who suffer from mental illnesses for the rest of my life. I will use whatever platform necessary to change lives for the better. Now I realize why various groups like Alcoholics Anonymous, MADD, and breast cancer survivors, etc. are so close-knit because they can relate to one another because they are in the same boat, so to speak. People who have certain illnesses or diseases prior to others can become a powerful and positive influence for a person who is "new" to a disease or illness. This is why many former drug addicts, for example, become some of the best counselors for current addicts. They know what's up!

MY CURRENT JOURNEY

ATTITUDE IS EVERYTHING

Although this has been very challenging for me, I have grown in so many areas in my life. It has taught me the power of meditation and how I can connect to my inner self. It has reminded me that I am a child of God and that I am always in good hands with his unconditional love. I have never felt sorry for myself and have never questioned, "Why is this happening to me"? I realize that some kind of mental illness plagues millions of people around the world and insomnia is very common as well, so what right do I have to complain about my challenges? I am learning to focus on the good things in my life, like my connection with God, my good health, my great marriage, my business, and my ability to persevere through tough times.

I have decided to focus on gratitude and self-acceptance. This is a learned skill that I practice daily using the meditation app. It is not easy, and it takes time to train our minds to focus on being kind and loving to ourselves because somehow most of us unknowingly berate ourselves and blame ourselves for our current lives, whether we are overweight, losing our hair, not having enough money, aging, etc. We even blame ourselves for having natural human emotions like sadness or loneliness, thinking that we should be happy and joyful all the time.

This constant judging of ourselves is one of the reasons that anxiety and depression is so common in our society today. Even on my toughest days when I was in a zombie-like fog, I would still joke around, be friendly, and say hello to others at the gym and the local supermarket and so on. Two of my favorite jokes were (1) when I leave this world, I seriously doubt that dying in my sleep will be the cause, and (2) I don't have to worry about what I am going to be on Halloween. That's easy—a zombie, of course!

I won't spend much more time on this subject for now, but I will mention it from time to time within my writings because I think that it can give people hope. Plus it's very therapeutic for me as well. I also realize that my type of mental illness cannot be cured; however, it can be managed to where people like me can live normal and productive lives.

LEVITATION THROUGH MEDITATION (SOME FINAL WORDS)

As you may know by now, meditation is an important aspect of my life. I started meditating out of necessity in 2017 because my doctor told me that meditation could be a way to calm the symptoms of anxiety. Since I was not sleeping well and I was desperate to try just about anything, I decided to give it a try. He recommended a free app that had various meditation practices. He also told me that for meditation to be effective, it would have to be practiced consistently. This was no problem for me since I knew that to succeed at anything and get the most out of something, it would have to be done on a persistent and consistent basis over an extended period of time.

I did exactly what the doctor ordered and began to meditate every day. Although I was still experiencing some of the symptoms of anxiety, the daily meditating helped. Even though I was nervous and stressed out at times, the meditation gave me a sense of calmness. I found a person by the name of Diane Yeo online who was a meditation instructor living in London, Ontario, Canada. Her free guided meditations were very helpful in introducing me to meditation. I also enrolled in a paid course in meditation by her that was fantastic. I would recommend her and all her programs to anyone, whether you are just getting started or you are very experienced. If interested, you can google Diane Yeo and her website will come up.

Shortly after finishing Diane Yeo's excellent program, I decided to take my meditation practice to a new level and purchased an app called Calm in December of 2017. Looking back now, I can see that

that was one of the best decisions that I have ever made in my life. Tamara Levitt, the founder and CEO of Calm, is a true inspiration to me and tens of thousands of people around the world. Her guided meditations are simply AWESOME! I have not missed one single day of hearing her soothing voice. My current total is 663 days in a row and counting. I have learned priceless lessons and ways to communicate with myself that I didn't think was possible. This experience has been truly life changing, and I have only just began to embark on this lifelong spiritual journey. I am truly experiencing "levitation through meditation." I have a saying that I use now that helps keep me on track: "When in doubt, exercise and meditate." Thanks, Tamara and Diane. YOU GO, GIRLS. Way to go!

Black Boy from the Barrio (Volume One) The Early Years

WHY THE BLACK BOY FROM THE BARRIO TITLE?

The reason that I came up with the title for this series of books is because Kim informed me that I did actually grow up in a barrio (Latino ghetto). It's funny how I never realized that I had grown up in a barrio and wasn't quite sure if she was accurate when she said that I had. But as I started to think about my neighborhood and what constitutes a "barrio," I knew she was right. Kevin Kostner produced a film a few years ago called *Mc Farland, USA*. My hometown, Earlimart, California, is about ten miles north of Mc Farland and are nearly identical communities. As I watched the movie, there was no doubt that I grew up in a barrio. I started to put together in my mind what makes a barrio a barrio.

I think a barrio consists of an area of people that are below the poverty line, at the poverty line, or are close to it. There are also drug dealers, violence, and crime. While growing up in Earlimart, I always knew that there was an underworld, but I was never involved in any of that stuff. I was too busy going to school, hanging out with my friends, and playing sports. Every once in a while, the "dark side" of the town would rear its ugly head, which I will get more into later. As a disclaimer, I will never use anyone's real name that might embarrass, shame, or incriminate them or their family, both past and present. However, I will be using both real and fictitious names in certain stories. If a story might seem a little controversial to me, I will be sure to ask permission from the person before I write it.

STORIES OF THE BARRIO

As I continue to write these books, I will tell many stories of my life growing up in the barrio. As an author, I will try my best to take you on a psychological journey to a place and time where things were different in some ways but are still the same today. The first few stories that I will write about is an opening memoir to show what a kid might be exposed to at a young age—first, growing up on an eighty-acre ranch then spending time in the barrio. So with that said, I think that the best place to start is at the beginning. So let's get started, shall we?

Black Boy from the Barrio (Past Events)

Cornelius Wright was born on the twenty-third of December in the year of 1960 in Bakersfield's Kern General Hospital. I'm the son of Clemetie and Dorothy Wright. At the time, I was the fifth child of theirs that would eventually grow to seven. I have four sisters and two brothers. Their names and nicknames are as follows: Arnetta (Netta), Wanda (Deeda), Terry (B. B.), Christine (Baylo), Cornelius (Neo), Charlotte (Lulu), and Antonio (Tony).

With seven kids in the family, it always proves to have interesting family dynamics. Now that I have gotten older, I realize that we all have a place and a space within the family unit. I'm sure that all my brothers and sisters have their own perspective on our family, and if you would interview them one by one, you would be amazed at what they would say. One of the things that I would like to do one day is to gather all the siblings and tell stories about our childhood. Not only would this bring about forgotten memories but it would also be interesting to hear the different viewpoints from all of us.

Clemetie and Dorothy met sometime in the early fifties in Bakersfield, California. They were part of the many African American families that moved out west from the South during the late forties and fifties. My father was the fourth child in a family of five children. He was a strikingly handsome man that was part African American and part white. They migrated from Altheimer, Arkansas, in the late forties by selling their farm. My mother was the fifteenth child of a family of sixteen from Bonita, Louisiana, that navigated to Bakersfield and Portland, Oregon, around that time.

My father would tell me stories of their family living at a place called the C. C. Ranch (outside of Bakersfield) where families would live in military-style barracks that the farmer owned. These makeshift homes were provided for the workers who worked in the fields all day. My dad would tell me stories about all the "riffraff" that would go on at the ranch. He called it a modern-day Peyton Place. He would tell me about how on weekends black people from all over California would come to the infamous C. C. Ranch for drinking, dancing, gambling, and prostitution. He told me that he saw many things that a young boy should not be exposed to. During his teenage years, he told me that an older woman from San Francisco who was a known sugar mama offered to take him back to the Bay Area with her. He declined, of course, being a true country boy.

On the weekends and after a hard week of manual labor working in the fields in one-hundred-degree heat, my father would drive to Bakersfield where he would go to some of the local "honkie-tonks" on the infamous Cottonwood Road for entertainment. He was not much of a drinker then, but he was definitely eye candy for many of the young girls that attended these places. He told me how he would party all night and get home just in time for work the next morning. "Get up out that bed," my grandfather would yell. "You been out all night like a tomcat and now you laying there stanking." My grandfather, Willie Wright, was a hardworking man that would not tolerate not showing up for work because you were too burned out from partying the previous night. My dad would tell me that he thought that his father was being hard on him. But later, my dad told me that he appreciated that his father was strict because it instilled a good work ethic in him that would last all his life.

After living at the C. C. Ranch for a few years, my grandparents were dismayed at the lifestyle in California. They thought selling the farm in Arkansas and moving out west would prove to be a much better living situation. But it was not. Dad would tell me throughout his life that they would have been better off if they had stayed in Arkansas. Who knows? The grass always seems to be greener on the other side of the fence.

THE BURTONS

My mother's childhood was somewhat different from my father's. She was the youngest girl in a family of sixteen. Her parents, Bruce and Mattie Burton, were from the swamplands of Louisiana. They also moved to California seeking a better life. The Burtons were a very vivacious loud-talking people that were blessed with the gift of gab. My mother would tell us kids about the Louisiana swamplands and the stories about water moccasins and giant spiders. She once said that her brother saw a spider that was "as big as a washtub" and her brother was afraid to shoot him, fearing that it would only make the spider mad. She would also tell us ghost stories about "hanks" and how they would see ghosts at the local cemetery.

When Bruce and Mattie moved out west, some of their kids, who were already grown, moved to Portland, Oregon. Many African American people moved up to the Pacific Northwest to work at the shipyards. My mother resided in Bakersfield with her parents. The siblings that stood out most in my mother's family (in my opinion) were Moses, Helen, Gene, Arthur, and Tony. Uncle Moses was a well-versed preacher as well as a businessman who owned a janitorial business in Bakersfield. Aunt Helen moved up to Portland, Oregon, and became a wealthy property owner. Uncle Gene was an uneducated construction laborer who did quite well for himself by investing in real estate. Uncle Arthur was a gregarious stutterer that would have you in stitches all day talking about his life and the stories of his military days and the time he spent at San Quentin. Uncle Tony was a hustler, plain and simple. He was the kind of person that was always on the move. He basically made his living by hustling on the streets. He was a quick-witted and a smooth-talking con man. My father said that Uncle Tony was so convincing that he could "talk a possum out of a tree with hound dogs on the ground waiting for him." I rest my case!

My mother and father met in the early fifties and started courting each other. They eventually got married and started a family. All of us kids were born in Bakersfield except for Tony, who was born in Delano, California, in 1969. After working for S. A. Camp and Sons in the late fifties, my dad was offered a job working for Vignolo Farms. C. J. (Ted) Vignolo was a former bookkeeper for S. A. Camp but had started his own farming company. Vignolo Farms had various ranches that spread throughout both Kern and Tulare Counties. Many of Ted's employees were living in homes that he owned that were surrounded by eighty-acre parcels of farmland. A situation like this was ideal for a man that had small children and that needed steady work. There was an eighty-acre ranch outside of Earlimart, California called the South Ranch. There were two houses and a barn on a two-acre lot that had its own water source. There were also two butane gas tanks that were used for the ovens inside both houses. There was a white wooden fence that circled around both houses as well. Various fruit trees like apples, apricots, and peaches were spread throughout the property too.

THE EARLY YEARS

The two earliest memories that I have in my life is first, the time that my uncle Booney was staring down at me when I was an infant. Since Uncle Booney died in 1962, I must have been only about one and a half years old. The memory of him was very vivid. I told my family members about this, and they did not believe me. The first time that I saw a picture of Uncle Booney was when I was about fifteen years old. We didn't have many family pictures in our household, but somehow my grandmother had kept an old photo of him and his wife, my aunt Honey. My grandmother (Mama Tina) had the picture enlarged and framed. When I saw the picture at age fifteen, I knew this was the man that was looking down at me in that crib earlier in my life.

My second earliest memory was the time that it snowed in 1962 in the Central Valley. I remember vividly the icicles hanging from the eaves of the front house at the South Ranch. I also remember the ground being covered with snow. A few of us kids went outside and made a snowman. I remember distinctly that the snowman was partly covered in grass since the snow hadn't completely covered everything. We rolled one big snowball for the snowman's body then rolled a baseball-sized snowball for his head.

My grandparents on my dad's side lived in a small town called Teviston, California. It was about two miles north of Earlimart. It was a very small community of mainly African Americans. My aunt Ossie Lee, aka Aunt Plute, lived in Teviston as well. I remember visiting their homes and playing with my grandfather's old push lawn mower. There was a high content of alkali in the dirt in Teviston, which made it a very fine powder. I would push the lawn mower through the dirt as fast as I could, thus making a small dust storm, which I thought was cool. The people living in Teviston nicknamed this place the Alkali. The Alkali was a quiet place by day; however, by nightfall, it would turn into a big party place. Like the C. C. Ranch that I mentioned before, the Alkali had gambling shacks, drinking, and prostitution. It was a place where blacks could meet and have fun on the hot summer nights of the Central Valley.

I remember a woman named Bert Lee, who I was told later by my father was the madam of the "juke joint" in the Alkali. Of course I did not know of all these happenings at the time because I was too young to understand it all. When I went to the Alkali, I was too busy having fun running to and from my grandparents' house and Mr. Drake's. Mr. Drake, aka Papa, was a friend of the family who was about 103 years old. He had a friend by the name of Jack Goodman who was deaf and could not talk. He was referred to as Dummy Jack. I was really thrilled to see the men that came out to "slop" the hogs. I would watch in amazement as they would fill half-decomposed barrels of table scraps with water and pour it in troughs for the pigs to devour. I will never forget the foul stench and watching those four-hundred-pound hogs fight over that nasty slop.

THE KIDS AT THE SOUTH RANCH

Growing up in a family of seven children on the eighty-acre farm, there was always something to do and always someone to play with. As a child, I usually played with Lu, Baylo, or Terry. Wanda and Netta, who were approaching their teens, usually did their own thing. I remember Netta spinning around in the kitchen, dancing to songs like "Natural High" and "So Very Hard to Go" by Bloodstone and Tower of Power. Those great tunes are forever ingrained in my memory and are still on my all-time favorite song list.

But we all got together at times and played games like "hop-scotch," "Mother, may I?" and "red light, green light." At night, we played a game in which we waited to see car headlights approaching from about a mile away then ran around the inside perimeter of the fence that surrounded both houses. If we got to the starting point before the car passed, we won. It was both exciting for us and good for our health.

Lu, Baylo, Terry, and I would sometimes go on walking trips around the area, discovering new things as kids often do. One of our favorite pastimes was taking the dogs on hunting trips and searching for Jackrabbits.

There were many families that were either cousins or friends of ours that were constantly at the South Ranch. They all had children that were our age, so we would always have plenty to do. Some would come by just for short visits, some would come by to spend the night, and some would stay for a few days.

Most of the kids visiting the South Ranch were from Daddy's side of the family. Uncle Booney and Aunt Honey had a big family in which some of the children were around the same age as Terry, Baylo, Lulu, and I. Their names were Ron Gene, Kenny, and Stan. Ron Gene was about Terry's age and Kenny and Stan were around my age. Ron Gene would come to visit in the summer, sometimes without Kenny and Stan. He would mainly hang around Terry, and I would tag along like a little brother tends to do. They would talk about girls and sex sometimes, and I would get an earful.

On one particular summer, we went to visit Cleo and Calvin Moore who lived in Teviston. I was really excited to be with these older boys. I remember being "a fly on the wall," not saying too much but soaking as much teenage boy talk as I could. I remember Ron Gene and Cleo arguing about how tough certain dogs were. Cleo and Calvin had a mean German shepherd that they thought could defeat just about any other dogs. Ron Gene, being from the hood in South Bakersfield, told them their German shepherd would get killed by some of the dogs from his neighborhood. He mentioned a certain type of dog with a huge head which we thought he called a "pet bull."

Cleo kind of laughed and said, "A pet bull?"

"Pit bull," Ron Gene corrected him.

Apparently, Ron Gene had witnessed many pit bull fights growing up in the hood. Cleo never had. It was the first time any of us, besides Ron Gene, had heard of such a dog. Trust me, it would not be the last.

I didn't understand the connection between Ron Gene, Cleo, and Calvin until I was around twelve years old. After the summer when we visited their house, they moved to Oklahoma. Cleo and Calvin's father's nickname was Sambo. There were two Sambos in the area. One was "Black Sambo" and the other one's name was "Red Sambo." Red Sambo was Cleo and Calvin's father.

After living in Oklahoma for about a year, we were told that Ron Gene would be living with them for a while. We never made the connection until after Ron Gene came back to Bakersfield a year later. Daddy finally told us that the reason Ron Gene moved to Oklahoma for a while was because Sambo was his father. Terry and I were shocked at first, but when we thought about it, it all started to make sense. Ron Gene was not a "Wright" by blood, just by name. It still felt kind of weird at first realizing that Ron Gene was Cleo and Calvin's biological brother.

Kenny and Stan were about the same age I was. To be exact, Kenny was a few months older and Stan was about a year younger. Although they were brothers, they couldn't be more different. Kenny was roguish like his father, Uncle Booney, and his older brothers, Darnell and Frankie. Stan was very mellow like his mother, Aunt Honey. We had a blast whenever they would come to the South Ranch for a couple of days in the summer. We all thought that we could run pretty fast, so we constantly lined up for foot races.

"On your march, set, go," we would say as we ran as fast as we could for about fifty to one hundred yards. Sometimes I would win; other times, Kenny or Stan would win. We had such a good time it didn't really matter.

I remember one time when Kenny's attitude came to the surface. Kenny, Stan, and I were playing a game of throwing rocks at one another when Kenny threw a rock that inadvertently hit Jewel's 1967 light-green Chevy Malibu. Jewel witnessed what had happened and asked Kenny to apologize.

"I ain't apologizing for sh#t," Kenny said.

Then Jewel, with a very stern voice, replied, "Who is this bad little boy?"

Kenny said, "None of yo' godd#mned business."

Jewel shook her head in disgust and went back inside her house. What Stan and I witnessed that day was Kenny just being Kenny.

Stan was always a mellow kid, a lot like me in some ways. However, he did one mischievous act as a kid that I will always remember. Lulu, Stan, and I were in the backyard on a hot summer day in 1972 when Stan grabbed an unripened peach from our peach tree. He threw it as hard as he could at an unsuspecting kitten that was sleeping on the grass. The rock-hard peach hit the kitten right in the stomach. The poor little cat sprung up in total shock, rising about a foot into the air. When it finally came down, it had a terrified look on its face as it started gasping for air.

After squirming for what seemed to be an eternity, the little feline's movements got slower and slower. Less than a minute later, she died right in front of our eyes. I picked up the limp body of this now deceased creature. We took it near the barn and dug a little grave for it. What started out as a fun afternoon of playing at the South Ranch ended in tragedy. All three of us were a little sad for the rest of that day.

Traci, Leslie, and Gabby

Traci, Leslie, and Gabby Bradford were the daughters of Curlee and Wilma Bradford. Curlee was Aunt Putes's oldest living son. Traci was the same age as I was and Leslie was about a year younger. Gabby was the youngest, about two years younger than Leslie. They would also visit the South Ranch in the summertime on occasion.

We played the same games with them that all of us kids would play. Many of our games involved marbles. Marbles came in all kinds of shapes and colors and could be collected by winning a variety of different types of games, either at school or at home. However, there was one game that rose above all the rest when it came to competition.

The Menacing Game of Five Holes

Five holes was our favorite because it took the most skill. We would dig four little holes that formed a square shape with the fifth hole in the middle. The objective was to get your marble to go into the four holes on the perimeter first. Then, to win the game, you had to get the marble into the center hole. If you did this, you would be able to keep all of the other participants' marbles. You could also knock the other players' marbles out of the way if they got in your path.

Sounds easy enough, right? Not! The basics of the game, from a theoretical standpoint, are simple and can be lots of fun. However, when you add the human element into it (Traci), it can get kind of messy.

Leslie and Gabby were not into the game of marbles, so they would either just watch or go do some other activity. Traci, on the other hand, loved to play. Now, there's an old saying that's used in competition and you might have heard it before: "You gotta have skin in the game." This simply means that when you play any particular game, you have to bring something to the table that has value, and if you lose it, it could have dire consequences for you unless your name is Traci Bradford. Let me explain.

Whoever played the game of five holes at the South Ranch would have an assortment of marbles, in which they owned. Personally, I had over one hundred at all times during my grade school years. Terry had a lot, Baylo and Lulu had a few, and whoever was visiting us at the South Ranch had their own share as well, except one person.

Traci would ask us to let her play with no marbles. "That's right, no marbles." She said that she didn't need any marbles. We wondered what the heck she was talking about until we saw the object that she would be using. We couldn't believe our eyes when she showed us: it was a peach. That's right, a peach. Not just an ordinary peach, but a green peach that was about five times the size of our small marbles.

Since she was visiting the South Ranch as a guest and a beloved cousin, we let her have her way and allowed her to play with this "peach." Terry and I kind of looked at each other and laughed under our breath, knowing that a peach wasn't even round, so how could anyone possibly use it in a game of marbles?

If anyone reading this has played marbles, there are two rules that must be adhered to. One, you have to "shoot" the marble by placing it between your thumb and your index finger. You would then squeeze it until it shot out. Two, you can never "fudge" the marble or give the marble extra power by moving your arm in a forward motion. Your hand must be stationary at all times or you would lose your turn to shoot.

Unless, of course, your name was Traci Bradford.

Traci had her own…let's just say, unique way of playing marbles. But the correct term would be closer to, well, "cheating." First of all, she would not shoot the "marble" (peach) in the traditional fashion. She would roll it like a bowling ball. Anyone else would be disqualified and not allowed to play, but not Traci Bradford. Somehow, Traci convinced us that she was new to this game and she didn't know how to shoot properly. Again, we let her slide because she was our guest and her presence was appreciated…and because we were short-handed on contestants.

What we witnessed that day playing five holes will always be remembered. Traci and I still have a laugh to this very day about what happened. Since Traci was allowed to use her "unique" style of playing, she cleaned us out that day. Not only did she win the game; she won a pocketful of some of our best and most precious marbles. Terry and I were furious. Today, when we talk about those days, we have a good laugh. All I can say is "Well done, Traci. You go, girl!"

Roy Lee and Lois

Roy Lee and Lois were the son and daughter of Uncle Q.T. Hooks and Aunt Tit. That's right, her nickname was "Tit," short for "Tittie." She got this name when she was a little girl living in Arkansas on a farm. Mama Tina and Daddy Wright had some goats in which they would milk. Aunt Tit (Willie May was her real name) loved to squeeze the udders of the goat and drink the sweet goat milk. They called the goat udders "sugar tits."

I don't know about your family, but we have some strange and sometimes funny nicknames. The thing that I like about nicknames is that they are usually started out as a term of endearment, with no harm intended.

Roy Lee was my age and Lois was Lulu's age, so they would visit from time to time. We would also visit their house, which was a ranch similar to the South Ranch. Uncle Q.T. worked as a mechanic for Vignolo Farms as well, which meant that he was provided a house in which to live. Their ranch was about thirty miles southeast of the South Ranch. It was closer to a town called Shafter, where Vignolo Farms was located. We ran up and down the hills of their ranch all day long.

Since Roy Lee and Lois were the only kids in their family, they always had plenty of toys to play with. They usually got new bicycles for Christmas, so we would ride them all over the vast acreage of their ranch. Uncle Q.T. would drive to different locations all day to service the tractors and other machinery. Aunt Tit was a housewife and stayed home to watch the kids.

Roy was a spoiled child who got just about everything he wished for. He had a bad temper that would sometimes get him into trouble. I still remember the time when we went to the Fresno Zoo. The zoo had a carnival area with fun rides and tasty snacks. Lulu and I joined Roy Lee and Lois that day. When it was time to go, Roy insisted that he wanted some popcorn. Uncle Q.T. told him no because it was getting late and it was time to go.

Roy started to have one of his temper tantrums and repeatedly shouted, "I want popcorn!"

As Uncle Q.T. stood his ground, Roy got livid. He started crying, screaming, and insisting that his father buy him that popcorn. After we finally got to the car, even after we got on the freeway to head home, Roy Lee still seemed intent on making everyone's life miserable.

Finally, Uncle Q.T. had enough. He said, "If you don't stop crying, I'll really give you something to cry about."

As Roy Lee continued his tirade, Uncle Q.T. pulled the car over at the next available exit. He opened the door to the 1963 white Ford Galaxy and grabbed Roy Lee's arm and pulled him from the car. He then reached for his leather belt from around his waist and started to whoop Roy Lee. As Roy Lee danced around, trying to avoid those "licks," Lulu, Lois, and I just kept quiet. I guess Uncle Q.T. was right when he told Roy Lee that if he didn't stop crying, he would give him something to cry about.

I must say that the rest of the trip home was much more pleasant. Roy Lee had indeed quieted down after his little encounter with Uncle Q.T. Even though I didn't like whoopings, Roy Lee kind of earned that one. As we got older, Roy Lee and I would joke about that fateful day. It seemed funny by then, but at the time it happened, there was nothing funny about it.

Randy, Raymond, and Freida

Randy, Raymond, and Freida are the last of the cousins that were part of the South Ranch kids. They were the children of Freddie and Geraldine Smith. Geraldine was Aunt Plute's oldest daughter. Randy and Raymond were about my age, and Freida was about three years younger. They lived outside of McFarland (like the Kevin Costner movie) in the mid-sixties. They would later move to Teviston on a few acres of land. Freddie and Geraldine always raised cows, which was a fun environment to experience as a kid.

When they visited, Lulu would play with Freida and I would play with Randy and Raymond. We would also meet at Aunt Plute's house on Oak Street and play games in the streets, like kickball and baseball. I remember playing baseball around the corner at Arroyo Brown's house. All of us kids had a great time playing in Earlimart, which seemed like a big city compared to our usual country environments.

I loved going to the Smith's house for sleepovers too. Randy, Raymond, and I would go on hiking excursions around their farm. We would look for horny toads, lizards, rabbits, or any other kind of animal that crawled, walked, or slithered. For us kids, Teviston was the happening place.

Neighbors at the South Ranch

Believe it or not, we had neighbors at the South Ranch. Now, I must say that the nearest ones were a half mile to the north and a half mile to the south, but nonetheless, they were our neighbors.

To the north were the Pagliarulos. They had a big pretty house surrounded by grape vineyards. John Pagliarulo was a small farmer with a wife and two kids, a boy and a girl. All the time I spent growing up at the South Ranch, I never got to cordially meet any of them. They were a very private family. However, we would see the son, Tony, riding his minibike from time to time on the dirt trails behind our house, about a quarter of a mile away.

To the south of us were the Stoberts. They moved into their house in 1970 from East Los Angeles. Their family consisted of four people. The parents were young and kind of "hip," meaning that they were free-spirited. They had an older daughter named Cathy and a son named Robert who was my age. Terry and I liked to visit their old Victorian-style house, with its separate room upstairs. Another reason for our frequent visits was Terry's little crush on Cathy.

Robert's bedroom was upstairs, so we got a kick out of seeing his collection of naughty cartoon posters, featuring Wild E. Coyote and the Roadrunner. If you ever watched that cartoon, you know that the poor Coyote never caught that smart-aleck Roadrunner. However, in this poster, not only did Wild E. catch him; he had the Roadrunner by his neck saying, "Now say 'beep beep,' son of a B#TCH!" We thought it was hilarious and quite risqué at the time. Robert had something called a "black light," which made the posters even more interesting. They had a pool table in the basement as well.

Robert and his family soon moved to Earlimart on Oak Street near Aunt Plute's and Mama Tina's house. Robert would tragically die at a very young age. I will explain how in a later chapter.

The Andersons

This story is not about "Mr. Anderson" in one of my all-time favorite movies called *The Matrix*, who, naturally, was nicknamed "Neo." This story is about our neighbors, the Anderson family.

The year was 1968. The Andersons lived about one mile to the northeast of the South Ranch. Dick Anderson, a farming superintendent, was hired from Southern California to run a walnut-growing company. Their house was owned by the company and rested on about sixty acres of land. Dick was in charge of planting walnut trees on those sixty acres. They had a nice house with an above-ground swimming pool. He had a wife and a son (Danny) who was Lulu's age.

Dick, who was very friendly and outgoing, came by to meet our family one day. He was riding a little Honda 70 with Danny on the back seat. Tall and slender with reddish-brown curly hair, Dick was quite a character. Danny was the spitting image of his father, Dick, with reddish-brown curly hair with plenty of freckles. He also was very outgoing and very opinionated. Since he was the only child living at home, he pretty much got his way with things. One might even say that he was spoiled. (I definitely would.)

Nevertheless, our two families connected very well. Danny was a good kid, and I liked him. He had a good heart. I think, as kids, we are a product of our environment and sometimes our parents make mistakes while raising us.

Soon after meeting Danny, I went over to visit him at his house. They had a large country-style house that was painted white. They had a nice lawn with big trees covering the property. They also had something that we definitely didn't have, and that was a swimming pool. In those days, swimming pools were something that rich white people owned. So going over to Danny's house and swimming was real cool—pun intended! The pool was about five feet deep and made out of plastic. You know the kind. Terry would sometimes come to visit as well, mainly to swim because he was a little older than us. He didn't hang out with us "little boys" often.

Danny's mother was a very nice brunette woman, a traditional housewife. She had an entirely different life before meeting Dick. Danny would always tell me about his two older brothers from a previous marriage. Their names were Randy and Rick Thilking and they were originally from Illinois. He showed me photos of them with their baseball uniforms on. Apparently, they were good.

Danny's bedroom was filled with sports memorabilia, and he had a collection of baseball cards. Terry and I thought that this was so cool since we didn't have anything remotely similar in our bedroom at the South Ranch. We had a rollaway bed in the living room, which in fact was not a bedroom at all. After visiting Danny's house a few times, I felt very privileged to have him as a friend.

Baseball at the South Ranch

I remember one summer day in 1969, Danny came to our house to play baseball. Terry, Danny, and I managed to gather up two more players, Baylo and Lulu. We were all having a good time when all of a sudden, Danny was called "out" when he thought that he was "safe." Terry had made the call and was not going to change his mind.

Danny got furious and said, "If that's the way you like it, I'm going home!"

Terry shouted, "Then go home!"

As Danny started to leave the South Ranch and head for home, I went to try to console him. We didn't have many visitors that summer, and it was a treat to have a friend come by to play with us. As I chatted with him, he calmed down and returned to the baseball game. Terry shook his head in disgust as Danny rejoined us.

As I got older and started to learn more about my personality, I realized that I have always been a person that didn't like conflict even when I was a child. I wanted everyone to get along. Terry, on the other hand, didn't give a "fat rat's a#s!" My amiable "Mr. Nice Guy" personality would haunt me sometimes during my childhood as well as adulthood. Unfortunately, some people will take "kindness" for weakness, and I've had to deal with that throughout my life. I still do.

However, over the years, I have done extensive studying in the world of different social styles and I have a great understanding of what makes people "tick." What I found out is that I am me, and I am not weak in any kind of way, nor is any other human being. We are just different in some ways, and that is what makes life exciting and interesting. So with that said, all I can say is "I LOVE ME SOME ME." I hope that you can say the same thing for yourself as well.

Three Hills and a Cloud of Dust

Since we are still talking about Danny Anderson, there are two more stories that I would like to tell about him. The first one involves him and Terry. The second one involves me, Lulu, and Danny.

As I mentioned before, Daddy had sold the Mini Honda for a bigger motorcycle. Terry was the only sibling that was brave enough to ride it. He would give us other kids rides, but none of us wanted to ride it ourselves. Anyway, Danny came by one day when we were riding the Honda 90. Lulu, Baylo, and I were taking turns as Terry would give us rides around the South Ranch. Then it was Danny's turn.

We watched as Terry and Danny sped away along the dirt trail parallel to the asphalt road. Daddy would remind us sometimes that he didn't want us riding on the main road because of the speeding cars. As they disappeared into the horizon, we went into the house for a little while to watch some TV. After about an hour, we started to wonder where Terry and Danny were. It was very unusual for Terry to be gone that long while riding the motorcycle. After about another half hour, we went outside to see if we could see them.

As we walked toward the road, we could see Terry walking on the dirt road about one hundred yards away, approaching us. He was pushing the motorcycle by hand. As he got closer, we noticed that he was dusty and appeared to be a little frazzled. Danny was nowhere in sight. The motorcycle handlebars were a little crooked and one of the foot pedals was bent. As he walked past us, he didn't say anything. He just went straight to the barn and left the motorcycle inside.

We never asked him what had happened, but we knew. Nothing was ever mentioned about that incident. We figured if Terry wanted us to know, he would tell us. As time went on, the motorcycle would sit in the barn for about a year. As I said before, Daddy ended up selling it to a friend in exchange for a car and some cash.

Within the next year or so, Terry finally came around and told me what had happened on that fateful day. While he was telling me the story, he was actually laughing. We all have things that happen in our lives that might seem tragic at the time but can be hilarious later.

He told me that he and Danny were riding along an unfamiliar dirt road that was near Danny's house. This dirt road had many small hills (about three feet tall) that could be a lot of fun for an experienced dirt bike rider. Unfortunately, Terry and Danny were neither. Terry told me that those little hills didn't look that daunting, so he decided to give them a try.

As Danny wrapped his arms around Terry's waist, they approached the first of the three little hills. Much to their surprise—or terror—the bike went airborne. Terry managed to land safely. They also quickly realized that this was a one-way ticket, meaning that while traveling about twenty miles per hour, you could not suddenly stop. The only way to make it safely to the other side was to face all three of the hills…and the second hill was coming up fast.

Like the first hill, the motorcycle went airborne. This time, however, they were about four feet off the ground, much higher with the added speed. As the bike descended, it started to turn sideways. As soon as they hit the ground, they bounced like a beach ball. Danny held on for dear life, his blue eyes as big as saucers. His butt lifted off the seat and his legs went flying into the air, almost parallel to the ground. Amazingly, Terry still managed to stay somewhat in control. By the time they reached the third and final hill, they realized that this motorcycle excursion might not end well.

As they got to the third hill, Danny's body was already halfway off the bike. Like the two previous hills before, they went airborne again. This time the motorcycle, which should have been facing due north, was facing northeast. Not good. Terry couldn't hold the bike in place this time. As the bike flipped over, Terry said he remembered Danny flying over him like one of those dummies that we used to watch on *The Three Stooges*.

They seemed like they were airborne forever, but they finally hit the ground. Terry was relieved that neither one of them was seriously injured. Lucky for them, the ground was mainly a mixture of soft dirt and sand.

Terry still tells us that story from time to time, and we still get a good laugh. There's a saying in pro football that was used back in the old days when running the football was prevalent. They would say "four yards and a cloud of dust." However, my brother Terry was part of a story called "three HILLS and a cloud of dust."

Danny's Dingaling

During that same summer, Lulu, Danny, and I went on a walk to the northwest end of the South Ranch. We took the dogs, Trixie and Bally Bally, on a jackrabbit hunting trip. There was nothing unusual about taking the dogs hunting. That was one of our favorite pastimes. However, on this particular afternoon, something kind of weird happened.

While the three of us were standing on a dirt road that ran between a grape vineyard, Danny did the unthinkable. He first took off his shirt to expose his bare chest, which was not that uncommon at the South Ranch in the midsummer heat. Then, for some reason, he felt compelled to take off his pants along with his underwear. He pulled his pants and drawers (drows, as we country folks called them) all the way to his ankles. By this time, he was almost totally naked.

I was totally shocked. Lulu, on the other hand, had a more, let's just say "curious" look on her face as she stared at his private parts. Danny was putting on quite a show, and he knew it. I still remember his grand finale, which will remain in South Ranch lore forever.

After pulling off his clothes and exposing his pale white skinny body, his penis got erect and stood at full attention. After he noticed it, he threw his arms up into the air and started to twist his hips back and forth. His erect penis was now "dangling" and slapping against his outer thighs. After about thirty seconds of exposing his "junk," he pulled his pants and underwear back up. Show's over. Back to hunting. Me and Lulu couldn't believe what this little redhead white boy was doing. In those days, sex and nudity were completely taboo for us. As I look back on Danny's devious little act today, all I can do is laugh. I guess Danny was quite the trailblazer.

Quentin Jones and Family

Quentin Jones was the son of Mama's best friend, Blanche Gibson. We met when Mama used to go up to visit Blanche in Teviston. I was about nine or ten years old at the time. Blanche was a robust dark-skinned woman who, like Mama, loved to chew tobacco. They were kind of kindred spirits. I believe that they met in Stockton (at the mental institution) during the time when Mama was having one of her psychotic episodes and was there for treatment. Blanche also had problems with mental illness during her lifetime. At the time, I was too young to understand what was going on as far as having a mental illness. However, I fully understand now since I have experienced mental illness myself. I will spend plenty of time in my memoirs discussing mental illnesses in future chapters.

Blanche's mother and father lived a few blocks northwest of Blanche in Teviston. Blanche's kids—including Quentin (my best friend at the time)—lived with Blanche's parents, Mr. and Mrs. Cooper. Quentin was the oldest of four siblings. He had three younger sisters named Wanda Mae Spears, Lillie Pearl Thomas, and Jeannie Woods.

Mrs. Cooper was a short heavyset woman with bowed legs. Mr. Cooper was tall and thin with only one eye. We never had the nerve to ask him what happened to his other eye, but I heard that he lost it in the war. Mr. Cooper was a very gregarious man who loved to talk. For some reason, he would call Quentin "brother." "Brotha, brotha," he would yell whenever he needed Quentin for something.

Baylo and Lulu would become best friends of Wanda Mae and Lillie Pearl. They are still very good friends today. Mama would take the three of us to visit them at least once every week during those years. We would spend the night sometimes and run the streets of Teviston, which was a happening place for kids our age. Quentin always had some neat toys to play with, and he always had a nice bicycle. Quentin, a big kid for his age, would sometimes let me ride on his bicycle with him. I would sit on the handlebars as he would pump the pedals.

One day while riding his bike together, his neighbor, Wendell Rhodes, was sitting on his front steps. Wendell was about four years older than we were, light-skinned with green eyes. Quentin would tease him at times and scurry away on his bike before Wendell could catch him.

One day, Quentin and I were riding his bike like we often did, with me on the handlebars. We were on the asphalt street in front of Wendell's house. Quentin yelled a teasing remark as we passed the seemingly empty house. All of a sudden, the front door flew open and Wendell—who could flat out book—started chasing us. We had about a fifty-yard lead on him when he busted out the door.

I remember Quentin saying, "No way this little negro gonna catch us." Quentin must have forgotten two things. One, I was riding with him this time, which made his usual successful getaways more complicated. Two, he didn't realize how fast and determined Wendell was.

Once Quentin realized that his bicycle was much slower with the added cargo (me), he knew that we were in trouble. As Quentin desperately tried to pump the pedals with all his might, Wendell only got closer. What started out as a joyride for me and Quentin all of a sudden became a nightmare. Wendell quickly caught us and violently grabbed the handlebars where I was sitting.

As he yanked them, Quentin and I couldn't help but to fall to the ground on the hot pavement. Wendell looked at Quentin and said, "I told you I was gonna get you, negro."

Seemingly relieved, he started to walk back to his house. Quentin and I managed to pick ourselves up off the ground and get back on the bike. Somehow after that incident, that joyful bike ride didn't seem as much fun as before, especially having skinned our knees and elbows. After that day, we learned a valuable lesson: "Never mess with a light-skinned negro with green eyes who could run like a deer."

Quentin and his family would also visit us at the South Ranch from time to time. Those were definitely some fun years.

Starting School
in the Barrio

I remember catching the school bus in front of our house at South Ranch in the midsixties. I was five years old at the time when our bus driver, whose name was Roy, would pick me up. We would drive all along the countryside picking up students who lived on the outskirts of town as well. After riding on the bus for about an hour, we would arrive at Earlimart Elementary School. Earlimart is a small town located in the Central Valley between Fresno and Bakersfield. Its population consists of about three thousand people who are mainly Chicano, with a few whites, blacks, and Filipinos. Most of the residents were field-workers, including our family. The name *Earlimart* came from early settlers who worked in the fields and owned farms. It had a reputation for having produce being ready for sale before other nearby towns, thus creating the name *Earlimart*, meaning "early to market." Coming to attend school in Earlimart from South Ranch seemed like an adventure, and Earlimart seemed to be like a major metropolis compared to the remoteness of South Ranch.

I remember starting kindergarten in the year 1966, and my teacher was Mrs. Albright. She was a middle-aged white woman with a warm and friendly demeanor. Her style of teaching was very effective in that she was always in control. She would allow us to be kids, yet at the same time, she would remind us who she was and that she was definitely in charge. My best friend was Maynard Goree and Howard Mouton. We were three "manish" little boys that were always laughing and talking in class. We were at nap time, and we would pretend we were sleeping as Mrs. Albright walked by us. As soon as she got past us, we would crawl on our knees and look up her

111

skirt. Never saw any booty though. Only stockings and a girdle. Also, we were constantly being sent to the "talking table" for punishment. We thought that being sent to the talking table was an honor of some kind and a notch in our belts. Kids in other classrooms were being spanked if they got out of line. As I think back to my kindergarten years, as far as I was concerned, Mrs. Albright was Mrs. Alright.

As the kindergarten year proceeded on, I started to make more friends. Gamaliel (Gil Aguilar) was the youngest boy in the huge Aguilar clan. He had about four or five older brothers that were considered good boys because they were very involved in their church. But to survive in the barrio setting of Earlimart, you had to have a tough side to you as well. The Aguilar boys had that too. Make no mistake about it! I have proof of that firsthand. Gil and I became good friends; however, one day for whatever reason, we got into an altercation in front of Aunt Plute's house. His cousin lived right across the street, so he and his brothers were there along with my brother Terry arguing about something trivial.

As the arguing continued, Gil and I started to shove each other. Before we knew it, we were both on the ground wrestling each other. No blows were ever thrown, but I realized pretty quickly that I was overmatched. Gil was shorter than I was but much more stocky, which meant that wrestling was definitely in his favor. After about a minute or two, we were separated. I was glad because I had had enough. There is nothing worse than fighting someone that is your equal (or in this case, more superior) who is relentless and who won't quit.

After Terry broke us apart, I could have kissed him because I was dog-tired. I had lost! Terry promised that he would get revenge on Gil's older brother, Obed, who was his same age. I never heard anything about their altercation until we were adults. Terry informed me that he and Obed did have a fight and that Obed was as tough as they came. He said that the outcome was a draw, meaning a tie. After that incident, we never had any more run-ins with the Aguilar boys. In fact, we became very good friends with no lasting animosity of our fights. This is how it works in the barrio. You have to stand your ground and show no sign of weakness, otherwise you would definitely be picked on.

BACK AT THE SOUTH RANCH

Meanwhile, at the South Ranch, everything seemed fine and normal as far as I was concerned, being a young boy growing up in the country. However, there was one thing that kind of bothered me. Daddy would get up early in the morning and get ready for work. Mama would reluctantly get up and fix his breakfast saying that he should fix his own breakfast. Heated arguments would occur over the years of their marriage stemming from this disagreement. As I look back to those years, I understand now why they were arguing so much about this situation. Mama and Daddy had different philosophical ideas about certain things because of their different upbringings. Daddy grew up in a traditional family, in which the husband would go to work and be the breadwinner and the wife would cater to his every need.

On the other hand, Mama grew up in a very large family in which everyone would share in household chores no matter what sex you were. Daddy believed he needed the moral support from her every morning to get his day started properly. As a small child, these arguments were deeply disturbing to me and my brothers and sisters. The arguments would sometimes end with Daddy sobbing then slamming the door in frustration. Hearing him cry was shocking for a young boy who was taught that crying was a sign of weakness.

As Daddy left the house and went outside, he would start his old work car and let it warm up. He had an old Plymouth that ran good enough for a second car in which he used for work. One time, his best friend Sonny Perry needed a car to get to work because his car was broken down. Daddy let Sonny use that old Plymouth for as long as he needed it. After that generous favor, Daddy and Sonny became best friends for the rest of their lives. Later in life, I would often hear Sonny express the appreciation for that favor that Daddy did for him way back in the sixties. I would sometimes hear him say, "Bew, I have never forgotten the favor that you did for me back then. That car was the reason that I was able to get to work, which meant that I was able to feed my family." Sonny was forever grateful.

WHEN KIDS CRY

For starters, I would like to say this is one of the hardest chapters that I will write about in this book. The late great performer Prince once had a song titled "When Doves Cry," The song was about the dysfunction between him and his parents. I, on the other hand, did not have many disagreements with my parents. They were in charge, and I knew it. Most of the time, I did what they said fearing that if I disobeyed them, I would get a whoopin'. Back in those days, it was kind of a one-way deal. Of course our relationships would change over the years, meaning we (especially Daddy) would become great friends that would know each other very well.

I thought that it would be important to write about this to show that everything was not peaches and cream while growing up at the South Ranch. Looking back now, I realize that we were a typical American family. However, when I was a kid, I was not quite so sure. Everyone else's families always looked so perfect—you know, kinda like *Mayberry R.F.D.* or the *Brady Bunch*.

I realized from an early age that Mama and Daddy would not agree on all things. As I explained earlier, there were some philosophical differences in the way that they thought stemming from their upbringings. It did not bother me so much when they were just bickering at each other like most couples do as long as they would not try to invite me into the fight and pick sides. Sound familiar? Anyway, some of the bickering turned into shouting matches that got very personal and, at times, got violent. Now there is something that I want to get straight before I continue. I want you guys to understand that my father was not a violent man. I believe that with my whole heart. In fact, throughout his life, he would constantly say, "I hate violence." There have been countless times in my life in which

I saw a very gentle man with a heart of gold. What I also saw was an unhappy man that was desperately searching for peace. He was in a situation (in life) in which he was not sure he could get through. Hopefully, you will understand more as you continue to read.

In all the verbal altercations that Mama and Daddy had during their lives, I can remember one or two times when they got physical. Daddy never hit Mama, but they got into (let's just say) a couple of wrestling matches before. Of course, when all this was happening, all of us kids were mortified. We were pleading for them to stop, which they eventually did. In many cases, men's and women's relationships were different back in those days as opposed to the current times. Many men were considered "he-men" and believed that they should rule their households with an iron fist. Our society taught them that they were the "kings" of the household and the women were the "queens." Also, they (the men) should have the final word on the household decision-making. Well, that all might sound good according to society's standards, but Mama was not having it. She was a spitfire who did not take sh#t!

There was one fight that I will call the fight of fights. In fact, it was so bad that I actually ran outside and hid in the cotton field. It was kind of odd because Mama was not even present at the time. Let me explain. Mama had been spending a lot of time with her best friend, Blanche Gibson. They were driving up to Tulare (which is about twenty miles north of Earlimart) just about every day. Apparently, Tulare had some single men that were always looking for women. Blanche, who was single, appeared to be interested in some of the guys in Tulare. However, Blanche did not drive, which meant she could not visit the men without Mama, who was her driver. Apparently, Daddy did not see it that way. He believed that the two of them were seeing men together. I remember Dad saying, "They up there seeing those no-good 'Tulare negroes.'" Apparently, Daddy believed that Mama was having an affair while he was at work all day. Of course later on this would not prove to be true, but it was a scary time in our history at the South Ranch.

A DOOR AND A GUN

I think that I was about nine or ten years old when all this drama was happening at the South Ranch, and I remember it vividly. One summer evening after Daddy got home from work, he noticed that the blue 1968 Chevy that he and Mama owned was nowhere to be seen. He figured that Mama and Blanche must be out carousing with those Tulare guys again. I remember him saying, "That's it. I've had it. I'm gonna put a stop to this sh#t for good." All of us kids were at home at the time, so we all felt the brunt of his anger. As we watched him march around the house cursing like a madman, we just kept quiet, hoping that none of his anger would come our way.

Then, he did something that will be burned in my memory for the rest of my life. He went to his bedroom closet and grabbed his twelve-gauge shotgun and placed it next to the front door. I want you to realize that most people living in rural areas had shotguns that were mostly used for hunting, so it was not unusual to have a shotgun in the house. Daddy would sometimes go jackrabbit hunting with friends, and on occasion, Terry and I would go out shooting as well. Terry did all the shooting because, at that age, I was afraid to shoot a gun with that much power. The recoil and kick from a twelve-gauge can be hazardous for a little boy of my age, or at least I thought that it might. Plus, the loud noise of that gun would spook me a little. All of us kids knew that the gun was off-limits, which meant that the shotgun was never touched by any of us, other than Terry on occasion.

After Daddy sat the gun next to the front door, he informed all of us that he was going to blow Mama's head off as soon as she walked through the front door. Of course this led to mass panic among us kids. As we stood there in shock, Netta cried and begged Daddy to not shoot Mama. I, along with my other siblings, just sat there in shock. We couldn't believe what was happening. After about a half hour of hoping that he would change his mind or that Mama would come back after he cooled off and went to bed, our worst nightmare came true. We could hear the faint sound of car tires rolling over the gravel driveway. We looked outside and saw the blue 1968 Chevy Impala coming to a halt.

After watching Mama get out of the car and start approaching the house, I could not take it anymore. I jetted out of the back door and ran as fast as I could into the cotton field. After about a quarter of a mile out, I laid down on the ground and covered my ears. I could barely stand to hear that shotgun blast when Terry was target practicing, let alone hearing that awful sound as it killed my mother. After staying out in that cotton field for about an hour, I figured that I might as well head back for the house. Much to my relief, Daddy had not shot Mama. In fact, it seemed pretty normal when I got back. Mama was in the kitchen making some fried chicken, and Daddy was sitting on the couch watching the evening news along with some of the other kids. However, there was one thing that I noticed immediately when I walked into the house. There was no shotgun leaning by the front door. Whew, what a relief.

Nothing about that awful evening would ever be discussed until I asked Daddy about it decades later. He said that he never intended to shoot Mama and that the gun was never loaded. "I just wanted to scare her," he said. He ended up apologizing to me for acting in that way and also deeply regretted some of his actions as a young man.

DADDY, ARE YOU OKAY?

As humans, there are times in our lives that we would like to forget certain events and just wish that they had never happened. Unfortunately, that is just not reality. The following story is another example of how life is not always perfect. Even being a child growing up in a loving family environment at the South Ranch, life can sometimes rear its ugly head.

In the late 1960s, when I was about eight or nine years old, Daddy took Terry and me to Earlimart to visit Mama Tina and Daddy Wright. There was nothing unusual about that; in fact, we loved visiting them as much as we could. Daddy Wright would always spoil us by giving us candy that he had in his hidden his chest of drawers. Like an animal that gets fed for the first time, we would continuously seek more of those delicious treats. So whenever Daddy or Mama would say that we were going to Earlimart to visit 1008 Oak Street, we would get excited. There was nothing particularly different about this late autumn day except that Uncle Benny had just gotten back from serving in the Vietnam War about a year prior to that day. He was trying to get his life back together after spending about two years in combat. He and some of his platoon members were blown off a tank after running over a land mine. He lost some hearing in one ear and had some shrapnel that would remain in his body for the rest of his life. He received the prestigious Purple Heart Medal for his services. Way to go, Uncle Benny!

Anyway, Uncle Benny had gotten married to a woman named Virgie that he had met in Bakersfield. Virgie had four kids prior to their marriage. Their names were Ricky, Vickie, Lance, and Lonnell.

They would also have a child of their own named Benny Jr. (aka Little Benny). They were about the same age as me and some of my siblings, so we would see them occasionally in Earlimart or at the South Ranch where they would visit sometimes. On this day, Uncle Benny had brought the kids up to Earlimart to play with us. Up to that point, there was nothing unusual about that day. We were running around and playing games like we normally did.

All of a Sudden

Then, all of a sudden, we heard two loud voices. One was from Daddy, and the other was from Uncle Benny. Apparently, Uncle Benny asked Daddy if he could borrow his 1968 Chevy Impala. Benny had a car called a Corvair at the time, which was not that flashy. I didn't know where he was headed, but wherever it was, the Corvair was not the car that he wanted to drive. He wanted Daddy's. Even at a young age, Daddy would always tell us that a car was not a thing to lend out to everyone. There was just too much risk. Daddy would later tell us that the only person that he would ever lend his car to was Sonny Perry, his best and trusted friend.

As Uncle Benny continued to beg and plead for Daddy's car to no avail, he started to get angry. He knew that Daddy was not going to budge. All of a sudden, an argument ensued. Daddy and Uncle Benny were throwing verbal jabs at each other. The whole scene was taking place in Aunt Plute's front yard. I must say that I wish that those jabs would have just stayed verbal, but they didn't. The arguing got so loud that Mama Tina and Daddy Wright would come from the comfort of their house in the back of the lot to the front yard. Aunt Plute immediately came out of her house as well. Terry, the other kids, and I were shocked as these two brothers had gotten to the point to where fisticuffs might occur.

Then it happened. For some reason Daddy Wright, who got in between them, hit Daddy with a punch that landed squarely on his nose. As the noise from the blow shook through our young bodies, we watched in horror as Daddy fell to the ground. He immediately got up and looked at Uncle Benny. While Daddy Wright took a step back, Uncle Benny put his fists up and stared at Daddy like a crazed prizefighter. Daddy followed suit and put his hands up as well, mainly from a self-defense standpoint. I remember vividly how Mama Tina cried out for her two sons to stop this heartbreaking act of violence. As she cried, the snuff juice from her mouth ran down her blouse. Aunt Plute, who was as tough as they come, shouted out, "Y'all negroes stop this sh#t!"

The fight got into another level of seriousness when Uncle Benny figured that he was overmatched by his older brother, who was indeed bigger and stronger than he was. At that point, Uncle Benny managed to find a steel pipe that was about three feet long. Daddy, realizing that the fight was not in his favor now, managed to find a straightening comb for his weapon. A straightening comb is used for straightening one's hair after being placed over an open flame, usually on a stovetop. Most of them have metal or wooden handles with steel forks. Perhaps it was lying on the ground and slipped out of Aunt Plute's hand through all the commotion. What happened next is another thing that will be forever forged in my memory. As the two brothers squared up for the ensuing battle, everyone else stood back, practically in a state of shock. We couldn't believe what was happening.

As Daddy and Uncle Benny got within striking distance of one another, Daddy made the first move. He swung the straightening comb with a vicious swipe toward Uncle Benny's head. Fortunately, Uncle Benny ducked in the nick of time. Then, with a vicious swing of his own, Uncle Benny swung the steel pipe toward Daddy's mid-section. Daddy had his hands protecting his face, which meant that his ribs were exposed. We heard a loud *whack* as the steel pipe hit Daddy's ribs. He immediately crumpled over from the vicious blow but did not fall to his feet. Somehow he managed to run toward Uncle Benny and wrestle him to the ground. Thank God the grown-ups were able to break up the fight by then. Daddy, who was visibly shaken and in a lot of pain, managed to stand up. There was a slight hint of blood running from his mouth. Terry and I could tell that he was injured, but just how bad? We wouldn't find out until later that night.

After the fight, I remember a couple of things that Daddy said. The first was that he told Daddy Wright that he would never talk to him again for hitting him in the face. And the second one was that he asked me and Terry why we didn't help him. We found that to be a curious thing to say since we were just little boys.

Another thing that I'll always remember about that terrible afternoon is what Uncle Benny's stepchildren said to me and Terry. They told us that their dad had "won." Even at that young age I could clearly see that there were no winners that day.

As the drama ended, Daddy told me and Terry to get in the car with him to go back to the South Ranch. As we headed home, I could see that Daddy was in a lot of pain. When we got to the house, Mama saw what was happening and immediately told Daddy that she was taking him to the hospital. They went to Delano Hospital, which was the closest hospital in the area. After about three hours, they were back at the South Ranch.

Daddy was still in a lot of pain. He had a bandage wrapped around his chest and midsection. He informed us that his x-ray had shown that he had four broken ribs and one cracked one. I remember him on his knees and leaning forward on a chair trying to ease the pain.

When we woke up the next morning, we realized that Daddy was not there. We asked Mama where he was. She told us that he went to work. What! We couldn't believe it. How could a man with broken ribs go to work and drive cotton pickers all day? He later told us that he was in so much pain from the broken ribs that some of his workmates had to help him climb up on the cotton picker and get him seated properly in order to drive it. He also told us that the next few days were some of the most challenging in his life because of the intense pain he was in. Every time he coughed or hit a bump while driving that merciless cotton picker, he tried his best to remain positive. In retrospect, I guess that he was truly a man's man or perhaps a man that was very dedicated to working for his family at all costs. As I got older, I would definitely realize that it was the latter as opposed to the former. Thanks, Daddy.

As the years passed, there were no grudges between Daddy and Daddy Wright. The two men had discussed that fateful day in our family's history and buried the hatchet. Since Benny was always deemed the little brother of the family and the weakest one, Daddy Wright said that he instinctively felt like he had to help Uncle Benny. Of course he admitted to Daddy that he felt terrible about the whole situation and that everything happened in a blur.

Daddy and Uncle Benny had a pretty good relationship for the rest of their lives. As I will explain in later chapters, Dad had forgiven Uncle Benny for that incident; however, he would never forget about it. Finally, I will explain later how Daddy's asking for my and Terry's help on that day impacted me in my teen years.

THE THREE AMIGOS

Daddy had two very good friends in Sonny Perry and Jack Wells. Sonny was a stout-built man who smoked a cigar and worked on the railroad systems throughout California. He and his wife, Clarice, had eight kids that were about the same age as we were. We would often visit their house in Teviston and play with the Perry kids. We would play the normal games that kids would play like Mother, may I? and tag. But since there was a mixture of young boys and young girls, we would also play mischievous games like "doctor" and "house." Of course no sexual contact was ever made, but as I look back now, I can see how sexuality and curiosity is a natural part of being human, even at a young age.

Tommy Joe Perry was Sonny's youngest son, and he was the spitting image of his father. He was brash, gregarious, and always the life of the party. Although he and I got along very well, we were very different in that I was more quiet and subdued than he was. The Perry kids ended up going to another school in the nearby city of Pixley. Teviston was located in between Earlimart and Pixley; therefore, parents had a choice of which school they would allow their kids to attend. Pixely and Earlimart were different in the fact that Pixley was indeed a city, which means it had its own police station and city hall. Earlimart, considered a town, had neither. Also, I considered Earlimart a barrio because of the large Chicano population. In those days, Pixley's population mainly consisted of white people.

Jack Wells was Daddy's other friend who would come with Sonny to visit him at the South Ranch. Jack lived in Pixley and had a small family that consisted of two boys and two girls. He was a blue-collar worker as well, working at a nearby factory that made chassis for delivery trucks. We never connected to Jack's kids in the

125

way that we connected with Sonny's kids. I am not sure why, but that was the case. Sonny and Jack would come to the South Ranch about once or twice every month and pick up Daddy and take him to Earlimart to have a cup of coffee at the local restaurant. I remember asking Daddy one time if I could come along. Daddy told me no because they would be talking "man talk." Of course this made me more curious than ever, and I was determined to discover what this man talk was all about. As I got older, I would discover what this man talk was. It was the same for them as it is with men today, including me. Simply put—sex, sports, money, and women! I was once told by someone that a man's anatomy consists of three things: a brain, a spinal column, and a d#ck! Oh what simple creatures we men are.

As Daddy, Sonny, and Jack continued to build their friendship, I was still a mannish little boy, meaning that I would show out and talk out of turn when grown-ups were around. As I continue to write this book and tell stories about my "hidden stage presence" (meaning that I am naturally an introvert), I have always had a hidden desire to get in front of people and act up and show out. Once I get started, it's hard to get me to stop. Flip Wilson was popular in those days, so I would get up and do "Flip Wilson" in front of people. If you have ever seen the *Flip Wilson Show*, you know that he was famous for dancing around and saying "Whoooooo."

On one warm summer night in 1968, Sonny and Jack were visiting at our house and all of us kids were hanging out in the living room listening to them tell stories. As fate would have it, I interrupted them and started to put on my own little show. I want you to realize that of all my brothers and sisters, I looked the most like Daddy. In fact, Jack would always refer to me as Little Bew. Bew was a nickname that Daddy got when he was a little boy. His older brother, Booney, who was also a little boy at the time, tried to call Daddy his "little brother" but could not pronounce it properly, thus calling him "little bewla." That's how the name Bew came about. With that being said, I was Jack's favorite.

So as I continued my little vaudeville act in front of everybody and began to shake my little booty, Daddy had seen enough. He started to reach for his belt (which was a morbid sight for any of us kids) to give me a whoopin'. But before he could grab me, Jack interrupted and said, "Please don't whoop him, Bew." For some reason, Daddy heard Jack's plea, and it stopped him before he tanned my little backside. After that night, Jack Wells was not only one of Daddy's best friends but he was also mine as well. Way to go, Jack!

Motorcycles at the South Ranch?

I still have a love affair today with motorcycles because we grew up riding them at the South Ranch. In a future book in this series, I will explain how a motorcycle changed the course of my life. So stay tuned. Jack Wells would often ride his motorcycle out to the South Ranch from his home in Pixely. He had a blue-and-white Honda 350, which seemed like a pretty big motorcycle back then. Our next-door neighbor Tony Pagliarulo, who lived half a mile up the street, had a minibike that he would ride along the dirt roads and dirt trails that were prevalent at the South Ranch.

In the summer of 1969, all of us kids were anxiously awaiting the arrival of Mama and Daddy from a trip to Delano, which is a small city about five miles south of the South Ranch. They had taken many trips to Delano previously, but this one in particular had more meaning. Earlier that summer, we had seen some friends of ours that had a mini Honda. A mini Honda was a small motorcycle that had all the bells and whistles of a regular motorcycle. Unlike a minibike, which was basically a lawnmower engine attached to a bike frame, a mini Honda had three speeds and an automatic clutch for shifting. Apparently, word had leaked out that Mama and Daddy were in Delano purchasing one for us kids. "Mama and Daddy gettin' a mini Honda for us"? I shouted. "I can't wait." And that is just what we did. All day. That was the longest five hours in my young life. Finally, after waiting of what seemed like an eternity, they arrived back at the South Ranch.

HELLO, MY PRETTY!

As Mama and Daddy pulled up in their 1968 Chevy Impala, all of us kids were waiting in anticipation for the big event. Daddy slowly got out the car and walked back to open the trunk. Then it happened! Bang! We could not believe what we were seeing. In Daddy's trunk of his car sat a brand-new Honda mini trail 50 CC motorcycle. The excitement level was equivalent to all the previous birthdays and Christmases put together.

Daddy pulled the little blue motorcycle out of the trunk and put it on its nobby little tires. After adjusting the handlebars, he straddled it and kick-started it from the lever coming from the engine. It sounded beautiful as Daddy revved up the little engine. Then he clicked it into first gear and took off around the dirt driveway that circled both of the houses at the South Ranch. Daddy gave each of us kids a ride, then he showed us how to operate it by ourselves. For the rest of that summer and the next, we were having the times of our lives on that little motorcycle.

GOODBYE, MY PRETTY

By the end of the following summer, we had noticed that our little motorcycle was not on the back porch area where we always kept it. What we did not know was that Daddy was trading the mini Honda in for a bigger Honda motorcycle. That bigger motorcycle turned out to be a Honda 90 CC. Unlike the cute little mini Honda that we had grown to love, this motorcycle was full-sized and seemed intimidating to small kids like us. The only sibling that would ride this new "blue monster" was Terry. Daddy would give us rides, which were fun, but it was just not the same as driving the little mini Honda ourselves. My cousin James Bradford, who lived in the front house, would "hotdog" on the motorcycle by poppin' wheelies and spinning doughnuts. After about a year, the motorcycle era at the South Ranch came to an end because of a not-so-thrilling event that I will talk about soon.

FLOODING AT THE SOUTH RANCH

Early in the morning in the winter of 1968, Netta looked outside the bedroom window and rushed to Mama and Daddy's room. She woke Daddy up and said, "Hey, Daddy, there's water in the front yard." Daddy knew that it had been raining constantly the last few days and figured that the water had caused some puddling. Nothing unusual, right? He told Netta to go back to bed and get some sleep. Then Netta looked out the window again and rushed to Mama and Daddy's room again. She told Daddy that there was a LOT of water in the front yard. Daddy figured that he'd better take a look just to prove to her that she was imagining the whole thing.

When he pulled back the curtain and looked outside, he couldn't believe what he saw. Not only was there a lot of water in the yard but there was a lot of water everywhere. In fact, all eighty acres of South Ranch seemed to be a raging river. Daddy immediately woke all of us kids and said, "Get dressed. We gotta go." Mama was awake by then as well and agreed that we all had better get moving. I took a look outside the window and couldn't believe my eyes. There was about two feet of water as far as the eye could see. The water was murky and moving fast like a river. It wasn't getting inside the house, but it was close. Terry and I wondered how we would get out of the house since there was so much water everywhere. Since it was a school day, Mama and Daddy made sure that we kids did our usual morning routine of getting ready for school. But we all knew that there was nothing normal about that morning.

It had rained for about two weeks straight, and the ground couldn't take any more moisture. There was a river about three-fourths of a mile north of the South Ranch called White River. It was a narrow man-made river that was about twenty feet wide and about twelve feet deep, and it started at the base of the Sierra Nevada Foothills. Its purpose was to capture the snow runoff and safely guide the water to the agricultural lands of the Central Valley. Every year up until then it worked really well, diverting the snow runoff in a systematic way. However, with all the extra snowfall in the Sierras and the constant two weeks of rainfall, White River was in peril. Apparently, the bridge portion that was Highway 99 was lower than the other bridges in the area, which meant that a lot of debris got caught and the water couldn't get by.

The water would eventually rise above the banks of the river and start spilling in the nearby fields, thus causing a flood. The water would soon make its way to Earlimart and flood the western part of the town. Earlimart has two freeway underpasses that are below ground level. These underpasses would play a significant role in saving the town from flood disaster. The eastern part of Earlimart was dry. Mama Tina's, Daddy Wright's, and Aunt Plute's property were safe since they lived on the east side. Their houses, which were on the same lot, was a brief respite for us before we went to school—that's right, SCHOOL! With all the chaos going on that morning, we thought that school would be cancelled for sure. We were wrong. Fortunately, (or unfortunately in a kid's mind) Earlimart Elementary and Junior High were at the northeast side of town, which meant that the floodwaters did not reach the pearly gates of those fine educational institutions. Darn, school was still in session.

The Aftermath

After school was over for the day, many of the townspeople, including me and some of my classmates, wandered over to the western part of Earlimart to get a glimpse of what was going on. The rain had stopped, and the breakage on White River had been fixed; so we were out of danger at that point. We could not believe our eyes when we saw two of the three overpasses were completely filled with floodwater. The third one was partially full. Apparently, a car was submerged in one of the overpasses. Fortunately, the driver was able to escape unharmed. After the eventful afternoon, we walked back to Aunt Plute's house where Mama was staying for the day. After Daddy got home from work, we all piled into his green-and-white 1958 Ford and headed back to a muddy South Ranch. The water had subsided, and we were able to get back to our regular lives, which meant more SCHOOL!

1008 OAK STREET

The address of Mama Tina and Daddy Wright's and Aunt Plute's homes was 1008 Oak Street in Earlimart, California. Aunt Plute had a wooden two-bedroom single-floor house that was located in the front portion of the lot. Mama Tina and Daddy Wright's house was a small wooden one-bedroom house that was located in the back part of the lot. They had moved to Earlimart from their previous residences in Teviston in the late sixties. They were co-owners of the property. The address of 1008 Oak Street was and still is a big part of our family's history. I will write about the current happenings in later chapters. But for now, I will write some stories about growing up there as a kid. Just as a reminder, I spent my first fourteen years living at the South Ranch. However, we kids spent a lot of time at 1008 Oak Street as well. We were always visiting Aunt Plute and Uncle Cobb (her husband) especially when Mama was gone to Stockton and dealing with her mental illness. Aunt Plute was a part-time guardian, which meant that we kids would stay at her house from time to time. We actually enjoyed going to the big city (big compared to the South Ranch) and playing with the locals. There were kids everywhere around the neighborhood to hang out with. We befriended many of them who are still friends of ours today. There are four families that we were close-knit to, and I would like to mention them.

No Loves Lost

The Loves were one of four other African American families that were living on Oak Street. They lived three houses to the south, near the end of the block. They had migrated to the Central Valley from Santa Rosa, California, which is about seventy-five miles north of San Francisco. Mr. and Mrs. Love had a pretty big family, which was not uncommon at all in those days. I remember them having a lot of boys. Their names were Joe, Artell, Eddie, Victor, and Clouse. They also had a sister named Ruthie. Clouse (who was two years older than I was) was the boy that was the closest to my age. The older boys were doing, well, "older boy stuff," which meant that they were definitely not hanging out with young "rusty-butt boys" like me and Clouse.

Eddie, who was about four years older than Clouse, loved to ride his big bike with a long "banana seat" on it all over town. I still remember him riding that bike with his shirt open and the wind blowing it like a kite. He was always riding fast and was a little reckless. One time he convinced me to take a ride with him down to the end of the block and back. He promised that he would not go fast. Reluctantly, I hopped on the back of the banana seat with my legs dangling in midair. Eddie (the daredevil) took off like "a bat out of hell" (as Daddy would often say) with me hanging on for dear life.

This was not a fun ride. As his open shirt flapped in my face, I suddenly realized that I was in Eddie's world now and I would be lucky if I could make it out alive. Then, one of the most dreaded things happened to me. It was something that most kids fear while being on a bike. As Eddie made a sharp turn, my right foot got caught in the back spokes. I immediately yelled out in pain as Eddie came to a screeching halt. Fortunately, my foot didn't get mangled up too bad. I was able to pry it out with not too much trouble. However, since I was barefooted (like I was most of the time) the top of my foot and my big toe was bleeding. It hurt a lot, but I did not cry! (which I will explain later why not) After that unfortunate incident, Eddie went about his business of riding his bike like a madman.

CLOUSE LOVE

Clouse Love and I used to hang out sometimes on Oak Street. Like I said earlier, he was two years older than I was, which meant that he was also a little bigger than me. I remember one time he and I was playing at their house. They had an old couch that was outside in the dirt driveway that their dog would lie on. The cushions were dusty and covered with dog hair. Clouse decided that he wanted to have a pillow fight, so he took one of the dirty cushions and hit me on the head. Clouse was kind of a rugged kid, so he liked to play rough, especially with a smaller boy like me. As the pillow hit my head, there was a big cloud of dust spewing from it. I just laughed because hitting me on the head usually was not a good idea since I was deemed hardheaded by Mama.

It's funny how labels stay with us sometimes. Mama used to say that I was hardheaded, so I took pride in having a hardhead. I would sometimes ram people and other objects with my head. I remember running into the back of Uncle Benny's white Ford Fairlane, which had two semi-sharp wings on the taillights. This was not intentional though. I was being chased by Terry one day while playing tag. As I was running, I kept looking back at him, not noticing the danger that was ensuing. As soon as I looked forward, *pow*, my forehead hit squarely on the pointy part of the taillight. I hit the ground immediately and grabbed my forehead. A big knot instantly rose up as I squirmed in pain. Again, I did not cry! I still see remnants of that knot still on my forehead today. With all that said, I finally realized that when Mama said that I was hardheaded, she meant that I was not a very good listener.

As Clouse started grinning after his mighty swing of the sofa cushion, I grabbed the other cushion and hit him squarely on his head. "How do you like that, negro?" I said as I started to grin as well. After that, a full-blown pillow fight started. He would whack me, then I would whack him back. We were having the time of our lives. It all ended when Clouse sandwiched me in between the two pillows and sat on top of me. After the dust cleared, he let me up. We both stared at each other and started laughing hysterically. If you can, imagine two black kids with white dust covering them from head to toe. Our eyes were red and our skin and hair was white. However, the funniest part (in which Clouse and I would remember and laugh about for years to come) was when we both smiled. Our teeth were covered in dust as well. As we looked at each other's brown teeth we thought to ourselves, *It doesn't get any better than this.*

The Moutons

The Moutons were another one of the African American families that spent some time on Oak Street. They were only living there for a year or two. I remember a grouchy old man named Freddie who was the grandfather of Homer Dee and Howard. He would come out on his front door steps sometimes and yell at us kids. I figured that he didn't like kids because he was never nice to any of us. I remember playing in their front yard one day with Homer and Howard, just to be surprised by Freddie, who sneaked up from behind me and told me to get out of his yard. As soon as I turned around, he hit me with the palm of his hand on my forehead. The blow knocked me back a few steps. Visibly stunned, all I could do was to leave the premises. He told me that I "betta not bring my little black a#s back to their house." From that day on, I never went back to that house again. What a grouch! Their mother's name was Mada. She was always very nice to me when I came over to play. However, after that incident with Ebebenezer Mouton, I would not get close to that house ever again.

Homer Dee was a pretty gregarious guy who liked to joke around a lot. He was a year older than Howard and I, so he kind of played the big brother role. Homer Dee would always speak about a city called Richmond. He always told harrowing stories about living there. The only Richmond that I ever heard of was Richmond, Virginia. I had learned about some of the states in school. I often wondered how they got all the way from the other side of the country to Earlimart. I finally realized that he was that he was talking about another Richmond that was in California. Mada told me one day that they would be driving up to Richmond. She said it was about a five-hour drive. I put two and two together and figured that I was thinking about the wrong Richmond.

Howard was kind of a mischievous little boy who was my age. He and I would do naughty things when we were at school. I'll get more into that when I talk about my early years in school.

VIOLA BROWN

Viola "Vi" Brown lived directly across the street from Aunt Plute's house. She and her husband, Joe, were also one of the four African American families that were living on Oak Street. Vi and Joe were a pretty quiet couple that minded their own business most of the time. However, they did have a Doberman pinscher mixed dog named Sporty. Sporty would run back and forth in their gated front yard barking at us kids whenever we were around.

Vi and Joe had an old man as a tenant named Julius, who loved the sauce. Now, I am not talking about a wholesome sauce such as spaghetti sauce or soy sauce. I am talking about cheap "hood wine" (aka white port, thunderbird, superchicken, and night train). Julius was a small and very frail man who was drunk most of the time. He was one of the first people in which I witnessed firsthand what alcohol really could do to a person. Trust me, while spending time on Oak Street, sadly, I would see it all too often. I'll show you what I mean in a little while in an upcoming story.

The Mercados

The Mercados lived across the street from the Loves. I remember Mr. Mercado being an older Filipino man. He was married to a Latina woman (Mexican) who seemed to be younger than he was. They had two daughters from a previous marriage named Norma and Sandra De Los Rios. Norma and Sandra were probably about the same age as Netta and Wanda, so I never got to know them that well. However, the rest of the kids (Mercados) were close to our age. There was Greg, whom we called Junior, who was one year older than I was. Then, there was Maribel, who was the same age as I was and who was a classmate of mine for many years. Veronica was their little sister who was about two or three years younger than we were. Finally, there was Robert, who was the same age as Tony. They are still good friends today.

The Mercados fit in very well with all of the other kids living on the block. We would play the typical kids games like hide-and-seek, hopscotch, and kickball. Junior had a big red bike that would rival that of Eddie Love's. He was different in the fact that he was not a daredevil, and he was very generous in letting us ride it sometimes. Way to go, Greg!

THE ALVAREZES

The Alvarezes lived directly next door to Aunt Plute, Mama Tina, and Daddy Wright. Mr. and Mrs. Alvarez were very nice people to whom we would know for decades. They had three boys and one girl. Juan was the oldest boy who was two grades ahead of me in school, which meant that he was Baylo's age. Gracie was the second child who had long black silky hair. She was about one year older than I was. Terry would tell me later on in life that he had a crush on her. Alvaro was next in line. He was the same age as Lulu, which made him almost my age. With our ages being so close, we became pretty good friends. Thomas (Tomas) was the little brother of the clan. He was probably around six or seven years younger than Alvaro, which made him a perfect playmate for Tony and Robert. I will spend more time in later chapters writing about our relationship with the Alvarezes since we were neighbors for so long. However, there is one story that I will include in this volume. Here goes!

A Junkyard Dog

The Alvarezes were wonderful neighbors in every sense of the word. They would always say hello and smile whenever we saw them. However, there was one thing—well one "big black thing"—that I didn't like about them. They had two dogs. The first dog's name was Lobo, which means "wolf" in Spanish. Lobo was brown with a few black hairs on his snoot. He was a very mellow dog that didn't need a leash, so he would run around his yard as well as venture down the street from time to time. Now, Earlimart is what I would refer to as a "dog town." Earlimart has always had a huge population of dogs. Most had owners, but there were many strays as well. In fact, my cousin, Roy Lee would sometimes call Earlimart, "Earlibark." Anyway, you get the picture. More on that later.

Lobo had another dog living on his property as well. However, the only thing he had in common with Lobo was that they were both canines. His yard mate Oso (Spanish for "bear") was what people would consider a "junkyard dog." Unlike Lobo, Oso had to be chained up 24/7. He could not even be taken for a walk with a leash. He was simply too mean. He was as big as a German shepherd with brown eyes and thick black fur. The only difference between a bear and him that I could see was that a bear was probably much more docile, which means that I would have probably much rather faced a bear. He was as mean as a sidewinder, and everyone in the barrio knew it.

While playing with other kids and safely in the safe confines of Aunt Plute's backyard, Oso would constantly bark at us from across the wire fence. This was no ordinary bark. He would put all his effort into his barks while moving his head around in a circular motion. He was about eighty pounds of pure and unadulterated MEAN! I have been around and seen plenty of dogs in my lifetime; however, I have never seen one as mean as Oso. Terry and I still tell stories today about that dog and the times that he got loose.

Oso "Unchained"

One of my favorite movies is called *Django Unchained* by Quentin Tarantino. However, in the story that I am about to tell now, Django, Quentin, Samuel L., and Leonardo couldn't have helped me and Terry on that day.

Terry and I were playing about a block north of Aunt Plute's house at our friends the Garcias. Tommy Garcia was the same age as I was, which was about 7 or 8 at the time. We were also in the same classroom at school, so we were pretty good friends. Tommy's older brother, Joe, who was Terry's age, had a purple ten-speed Schwinn bicycle with a banana seat and a big gear lever on it. Needless to say, it was nice. Joe said that Terry and I were welcome to take it for a spin if we wanted to. Of course we said yes.

I jumped on the back of the banana seat as Terry got in front and grabbed the handlebars. Since Joe and Tommy lived on Oak Street as well, we figured not to venture off course and head toward Aunt Plute's house. As I look back at that day in the present time, I realized that heading down Oak Street toward Aunt Plute's house was the worst thing that we could have done. Why, you might wonder? Because as we joyfully rode that amazing bike toward Aunt Plute's house, the unimaginable happened. Oso got loose! Now, this was not just an ordinary dog that got loose and might try to run away to attain its freedom. This was Oso. The best way I could describe this awful situation is by remembering a movie that I saw in 1980. The movie was called *An American Werewolf in London*. The werewolf in that movie was a rabid, enraged creature that had no boundaries as far as somehow being tamed by humankind. It would bite or eat anything that got in its way. Oso was no different.

By the time Oso got out of his yard, Terry and I were just getting to Aunt Plute's, which meant we were the first victims on his list of destruction. With a broken chain and a cloud of dust, he hurled his body toward our bicycle, thus knocking both of us completely on the ground. He immediately started biting Terry's right leg. Lucky for Terry, he had a pair of Levi's on that managed to be his savior. Terry got up to his feet quickly and started to kick at Oso. Oso continued to hold on to Terry's pant leg while shaking his head violently. By this time, Mr. Alvarez and Juan had come to intervene. They yelled at the top of their lungs in order for him to stop. He finally did. But Oso was not finished. Not even close. After letting a terrified Terry go, he sprinted to Vi and Joe Brown's house, which was directly across the street from Aunt Plute's. He jumped the fence, which was about five feet tall, and continued his tirade at their house. By that time, the whole neighborhood heard the commotion. The Alvarezes advised everyone to stay in their yards and not come into the street. They certainly didn't have to tell me and Terry twice. We were already in the safe confines of Aunt Plute's front yard after narrowly escaping this rogue creature's vicious jaws.

As we nervously looked across the street to the Brown's house, we saw Oso chasing Vi and Joe's dog, Sporty. Vi and Joe wisely stayed on their front porch area, which was enclosed, as Oso started to attack Sporty. Dogs are usually territorial, especially in their own domains. However, Sporty didn't want any part of this dangerous canine. Sporty ended up leaping over his own fence and sprinting away down the street with a terrified look on his face and his little tail pointing down. If Sporty could talk, I could imagine him saying, "I don't give a da#m about all this sh#t that I hear about us dogs supposing to be the protectors of our owner's houses. That might be true for some dogs, but as for me, I'm trying to save my own a#s from that crazy motherf#cka." All the other dogs on the block were at high alert as well and stayed in their yards. This was definitely DEFCON 5, doggy style.

Finally, Mr. Alvarez and Juan were able to grab Oso's chain and calm him down. As they opened their gate and took him to their backyard, there was a big sigh of relief on the faces of all of us, including Sporty.

I'll Drink to That!

While visiting and later living at 1008 Oak Street, I witnessed the perils of the excessive use of drinking alcohol. Like Daddy growing up on the labor camp as a young boy, I, too, saw some things that a young boy should not have seen. When we used to visit our relatives at 1008 Oak Street, it would mainly be me and Terry. Since we were somewhat close in age and we were boys, we naturally hung around each other the most. Daddy would take us to visit Mama Tina and Daddy Wright probably about once a week. Daddy Wright was the handyman of the premises. He would always have a garden with ripe red tomatoes in the summer time that we feasted on. He planted two mulberry trees that still exist today. I remembering him laying gravel on the dirt driveway, thus making it more car friendly, especially during the rainy season. He also installed a shower in their bathroom. We had never taken a shower before (only baths) up to that time. So taking a shower at their house on occasion was indeed a treat for two "rusty-foot black boys." Daddy Wright also planted some grass in their front yard along with some concrete steps for walking up to the porch. I must say that Daddy Wright had that old house and that once beaten-down lot looking good. Mama Tina would take care of the inside of the house. She kept a very clean house and was a very good cook. With the both of them doing their respective household duties, their home looked great. Way to go, Mama Tina and Daddy Wright!

Aunt Plute lived in the front house with her husband, Harold Cobb. Uncle Cobb was Aunt Plute's second marriage. They had a daughter named Halean, who was about two years older than Netta. Aunt Plute was a "high yella" (light-skinned) woman who was the salt of the earth. She had a great personality, loved just about everyone, but did not take sh#t from anyone. There will be more very interesting stories about her in upcoming chapters. Just as a teaser, I'll let you in on a little information about her. Everyone knew that she carried a knife in her "boosome" (bra) and would not hesitate one bit to use it if you crossed her. She had a saying that I heard more than once concerning her knife. She would say, "Negro, I'll cut you as long as you live." So don't mess with Plute!

Uncle Cobb was a very tall dark-skinned man who stood about six feet, four inches tall. He had a problem with alcohol. He and Julius across the street were very similar in the fact that alcohol had taken a serious toll on them. Who knows what led them to drink, but even at that young, I thought it was kind of sad to see them drunk most of the time. Although I am a naturally positive person and try to shine a bright light on most people, there are times when it's hard to do. It's just a reality of life. Uncle Cobb and Julius were the first people that I knew in which I witnessed the dangers of excessive alcohol consumption. There were not many times when they were not drunk. Daddy would tell me stories when Cobb, as they called him, was a very strong man who would work in the grape fields all day and "swamp" (throw) grape boxes like they were lightweight rag dolls. Daddy said that Cobb was a "helluva man" when he was younger. I found that hard to believe from the shell of a man that I saw. Looking back, I have nothing but love and empathy for Uncle Cobb because I got a small glimpse of alcohol abuse in my twenties. It can be a runaway train if you are not careful. Luckily, I was able to break that terrible addiction. More on that later.

There was one thing that Uncle Cobb did better than any person that I've ever seen in my entire life, and that was eating fish. That was his "claim to fame," especially within our family unit. Now, I know that this sounds kind of strange, but to this day, I have never seen anyone put half of a bluegill perch, with all those tiny bones, in their mouth and start chomping away. Most people would get the fish bones caught in their throat. However, Uncle Cobb would start slowly chewing the big piece fish on one side of his mouth and have the bones come out the other side. Amazing! After that, he would reach in his back pocket and wash it down with some white port. Way to go, Uncle Cobb!

MUCHACHO, NEGRO!

We had a lot of fun and a lot of good memories while spending time at 1008 Oak Street in the 1960's. However, there were a few events that I would like to forget. Here's one in particular. Terry and I were in the middle of the street playing with one of the greatest toys that was ever invented. No, it was not a big wheel or a hula hoop; however, those would be good guesses. It was a Frisbee. We had found an orange Frisbee in the grape field that was at the south end of the block. Back in those days, when you found a toy or something, you would just play with it. Trying to find the rightful owner never crossed our minds. Finders keepers, right? Anyway, it didn't take me and Terry very long to find out how this toy worked. I guess Hasbro, the manufacturer of the Frisbee, did a fantastic job of marketing its product with all those television commercials that they were running all the time.

As me and Terry flung the plastic saucer back and forth to each other, a Latina woman, who had relatives across the street and with a newborn baby in a stroller, seemed to appear out of nowhere. I guess our young little minds were so engaged in having fun with our new "super toy" that we didn't even notice her. She parked the stroller outside the fence and was chatting with one of her relatives. Terry and I were still in the street throwing the Frisbee. After I caught it, it was, of course, my turn to sling it back to Terry.

For some reason, as I slung the Frisbee this time, it somehow got caught up on one of my fingers. That awkward release led to the Frisbee going in a direction in which I had not intended. Yes, you guessed it. It was headed directly to the woman and her baby carriage. All of a sudden, our time of fun on Oak Street was about to be not so fun anymore. The Frisbee slammed into the side of the carriage, thus waking the infant who was sound asleep. The loud cry of a newborn pierced through our veins as we stood there in silence. Then, all of a sudden, the mother who was visibly upset, yelled out some words that I still remember today. "Muchacho, negro [black boy]!" she screamed as she tended to her newborn after giving us the evil eye. After that interesting little incident, Terry and I picked up our new Frisbee and went into Aunt Plute's front yard and took a well-needed break. Sorry, Hasbro, no more Frisbee tossing for the rest of that day.

OH BOY, PO' BOY!

As strange as it may seem, there was one event that Terry and I looked forward to, and that was getting a haircut. Every so often, Daddy would load us up in the car and take us to Pixley, which was about five miles north of Teviston. Pixley was smaller than Earlimart, which had only three thousand people. However, Pixley had mostly white people living there during those times. There were a few African American families scattered about, but the population was mainly white.

Besides Daddy's good buddy Jack Well's family, there was another African American family living across the street from him. The family was made up of four people: a father, his wife, and two daughters. The daughters were older than me and Terry, so we would not see them too often. The wife would be gone most of the time as well. However, there was one person that we always saw when we got there. His name was Reverend "Po'Boy" Barkus. Po'Boy was short in stature, about five feet, four inches tall. He was dark-skinned and had a bald head. He had a very boisterous voice that seemed like a perfect fit for preaching the gospel.

After my nappy hair became almost uncombable, Mama insisted that Daddy take us to see Po'Boy. At that particular time during my young life (about five or six years old), Mama still would comb my hair sometimes when I would do a half-a#sed job myself. I used to hate it when she combed my hair. She was what I call "Louisiana rough." She would seemingly lift my little booty off the chair trying to get that comb through it. Tears would start to run down my eyes, especially when she got in my "kitchen" (the area in the back of my head around my neck).

I also liked going to Po'Boy's because it was a time of bonding for us guys in the family. I would not realize until later in life how important those times were for building a good healthy family chemistry that would last over time. Once we got to Po'Boy's house, he always greeted us warmly with his distinct low voice. We would enter the front porch area, which was enclosed. He had an old barber's chair near the corner of the room and some additional chairs for guests who would be waiting for their turn.

Terry or I, in no certain order, would jump on the barber's chair and let Po'Boy do his thing. There were never any other patrons waiting in line, so we never had to wait. Daddy would sit there and talk about all kinds of things with Po'Boy. This was me and Terry's first introduction to "barbershop talk." We would sit there snickering and smiling while we listened to the local gossip. Of course men don't gossip, right? We simply just state the true facts of the matter to other men. And oh, by the way, I also have some cheap land to sell you.

As Po'Boy started to cut our hair, he would always ask Daddy how low he should cut it. This always made us a little nervous because we were at the mercy of Daddy's decision. Most of the time he would tell Po'Boy to cut it low, and I mean real low. This type of haircut was called a covatis or something like that. All I know is that when we left Po'Boy's house, our "naturals," which were cool back then, would be sprawled across Po'Boy's floor for eternity. How sad.

It was sometimes shocking to me when I rubbed my hand across my head only to feel a bald head. It was even worse when I looked into the car mirror and saw it firsthand. For some reason, Terry's haircut was never cut as low as mine. Since my hair was considered "bad," I am sure that Daddy told Po'Boy to cut mine as low as possible. I remember riding in the car and heading back to the South Ranch. It was fun and very refreshing when Daddy would let us hang our heads out the window to remove any loose hair that might be on our heads. Even though I didn't like those short haircuts, I still really cherished haircut days. When we got back to the South Ranch, I was sometimes teased mercilessly by my siblings, including Terry, who would call me "bald headed." The others would call me names like "picked chicken" or "egghead." I didn't mind because despite all their jabbering, I still loved going to Po'Boy's.

BAD HAIR

Since I am on the subject of hair and haircuts, one of the things that I found out early on in my life was that all hair is not created equally, especially according to most people in the black community. Kinky or coarse hair is called nappy, which is a derogatory term. Black people with curly or straight hair are considered more attractive, especially if they are "high yellow" or light-skinned. It took me many years into my adult life to finally appreciate what God had given me as far as my hair. I had always hated that I was the only one in my family that had inherited my mother's hair. The rest of my brothers and sisters had a combination of both parents' hair, thus making it manageable and easy to comb. My hair, on the other hand, was rough and coarse. Yes, I had to accept the fact that my hair was indeed NAPPY.

Daddy's hair was considered "good" because it was curly and soft. I used to watch in envy as he just rubbed a little water on his hair and scalp and combed in with a fine-tooth comb. On the other hand, my hair was okay as long as it was cut short. But as it started to grow, it would start to kink up and become extremely difficult to comb. Thank goodness someone invented the Afro fork, which was a comb with spread-out teeth that would make combing my hair a little easier. The hard part in all this was that in the seventies, it was cool to have an Afro; and of course, I wanted to be cool, so I let my hair grow as long as it would grow. I still was never able to grow a big Afro because my hair was just too nappy.

I became a little more self-conscious about my hair as I continued to hear bad hair jokes throughout the black community. For instance, sometimes when Mama would get mad at me, she would yell, "Boy, you as bad as yo hair." As I look back at that statement now in my adult life, all I can do is laugh. I must admit that was pretty funny. Uncle Benny once told a joke that went something like this: "Negro, yo hair is so bad you gotta tie it up at night so it won't go rob people." I must admit, that was pretty funny too. "Curls for the girls" and "naps for the saps" became popular during my high school years. Back in the fifties, blacks would use a hair product called Konk. Konk or Konkaline was used to straighten kinky hair. However, if used improperly, it could burn the skin. There was a saying about the Konkaline product that went something like this, "If yo hair is short and nappy, Konkaline will make it happy."

As I have gotten older, I have learned to appreciate my nappy hair. In fact, I actually have good hair because I still have it all and it's not very grey. I would definitely call that "good hair."

MELWOOD PLACE

The only thing that Melrose Place and Melwood Place have in common is that the first three letters—*Mel*—are the same. Other than that, they could not be more different. *Melrose Place* was a television series about some young adults living in a swanky apartment complex in Los Angeles. The Melwood Place that I will be writing about is the one in Bakersfield, California. Actually, it's called Melwood Street, which sounds like Melrose Place, kind of. Anyway, you get the picture. To further clarify this, let's just call it "Melwood in the Hood."

While living at the South Ranch, all of us kids would go to Bakersfield with Mama and Daddy to visit our first cousins that lived on the south side of Bakersfield. The south side of Bakersfield was definitely considered the hood. As I said before, it was well-known for the infamous Cottonwood Road. Cottonwood Road was a place where many blacks would hang out and party. There were gambling joints, dance clubs, and prostitution. Mama and Daddy both would tell us stories about that infamous place and how people partied at those honky-tonks.

Uncle Eugene (aka Gene) and Aunt Honey lived about halfway down the block on Melwood Street. We would mainly visit them in the summertime. Uncle Gene, who was Mama's brother, married Aunt Honey, who was previously married to Daddy's brother, Frank (aka Booney) Wright. I know it sounds confusing, but there's no way that I can make this up. Uncle Booney died of a massive heart attack at the age of thirty-six. They had nine kids in which many of them were the same ages that we were. I would play with Kenny and Stan most of the time since we were about the same age. Terry would hang out with Ron Gene while Netta and Wanda would play with Debra and Brenda. Baylo and Lulu would roam in between all of us, not letting the fun pass them by.

I never saw much of Frankie, who was the oldest boy. I believe he was living with his girlfriend at the time. Now, Darnell, who was the second-oldest boy, was an entirely different story. Darnell was always somewhere in the vicinity of Melwood Street; however, he would be gone in the daytime. On many occasions, Kenny, Stan, and I would hear the sound of a fight at or near the end of the block. It was usually around dusk-dark or at nighttime. We would run down the street to see what the commotion was. Before getting to the small crowd of people, we would hear Darnell's distinct voice right in the middle of the fight. "Negro, I'll knock you out," he would yell out at the top of his lungs. I must say that Darnell was the most roguish person that I had ever met up until then. However, I will be writing a story later on about the life of Darnell that will simply knock your socks off.

WHAT UP, BLOOD?

I remember playing softball on Melwood Street one summer in 1968. Terry, Baylo, Lulu, and I were playing with some of our first cousins, which included Debra, Ron Gene, Kenny, and Stan. We were playing on a vacant sandlot that was next door to Aunt Honey and Uncle Gene's house. Everything was going well as planned. We were having a great time as most kids do when playing softball. Then all of a sudden, what had been a good time turned into chaos.

Terry got up to bat and hit the ball a pretty far distance. He sprinted around the makeshift bases (which were grocery bags with rocks on top of them to hold them in place) and was headed home for an apparent "in the park" home run. While rounding third base and heading for home, he suddenly stopped dead in his tracks and grabbed for his foot. I must note that we were all barefooted. In those days, we hardly wore shoes, especially in the summer months. Our feet were tough and calloused from running in the streets and skidding on the dirt all the time.

As soon as Terry grabbed his ankle, blood started to squirt from the bottom of his heel like a gusher. Apparently, there was a broken piece of glass that was hidden under the sand. As soon as he went down, everyone circled around him with concerned looks on their faces. As Terry writhed in pain, Ron Gene and Debra ran next door to tell Mama and Daddy. Within a flash, they were there to attend to their wounded son. In those days, no one would call 911 for an emergency. I am not sure if 911 even existed back then, to be honest. Anyway, as Terry lay there bleeding like a "stuck pig," Daddy lifted him up and had him stand on one leg. Uncle Gene, who was now on the scene, wrapped and old rag around his bloody foot. I got a glimpse of Terry's bloody heel before Uncle Gene wrapped it. It was not a pretty sight. I witnessed the biggest and deepest cut that I had ever seen up until that point in my life. It was about five inches long and seemed to go almost to the bone. I definitely saw "white meat."

Terry was swiftly loaded into the car and rushed to Kern General Hospital. For the next four hours, we kids sat around nervously awaiting his return. For what seemed like an eternity, Mama and Daddy finally returned with Terry in the back seat. There were a pair of crutches next to him. His entire foot was bandaged, and his heel area appeared to be swollen. As he got out of the car and onto the crutches, we watched as he limped his way into the house.

Of course we kids were very curious to hear about his harrowing story of being at a hospital for the very first time. Terry did not disappoint. He told us how he was admitted into the emergency section of the hospital. They quickly wheeled him into a room where a doctor was waiting. After examining the wound, the doctor had his nursing assistant get a hypodermic needle. Terry said he couldn't believe how long that needle was. Terry, who had been given vaccination shots many times before, prepared to be given a shot in his arm or perhaps his buttocks. When the doctor grabbed his ankle and lifted his leg to a horizontal position, Terry wondered what was happening. Then, all of a sudden, he started to figure out what was about to happen—the unimaginable.

As the nurse aimed the humongous needle toward his open wound, Terry said that he started to get a little light-headed. As the needle penetrated his tender flesh, he let out a loud cry. Apparently, the shot was given directly into the wound. Terry said the pain was excruciating. After the ordeal with the needle, they had him wait for about ten minutes. As he waited, he told us that the pain had vanished. Obviously, this was his first experience with a local anesthetic. After waiting about ten minutes, the doctor and the nurse returned to the room. This time, the nurse was carrying what seemed to be a needle and thread. They had him lie on a table facedown. Terry said he knew exactly what was going on by then. After his initial nervousness, he said that it wasn't that bad. In fact, he didn't feel any pain at all.

After we got back to the South Ranch after that long day and unbeknownst to Mama and Daddy, Terry unwrapped the bandage to show us his stitches. In a weird way, Terry was kinda the "kid of the hour," which meant that he got a lot of attention. I think he sort of liked that. But given the chance again, I am sure that he would not want to get attention by all that he had been through on that hot summer day.

UNCLE GENE

Since I will be writing about the subject of CHOICES at times in my books, I would like to tell a short story about a person that was not educated in school and could not read or write but was able to live a good life through good choices, hard work, and vision. His name was Eugene Burton, aka Uncle Gene. The best way to explain who Uncle Gene is, is to say that he was a devoted family man. He was very gregarious and loved to talk. He definitely had that Burton gift of gab. Uncle Gene was the hardest-working laborer that I had ever seen. My dad had told me of the legendary reputation that he had created working in the fields of the Central Valley. He was working as a field laborer for S. A. Camp, and his job was to move irrigation sprinkler lines. Moving sprinkler lines was a very physically demanding job. My cousin Roy and I had a summer job moving sprinkler lines in Delano, so I know firsthand that the work is not easy. Sprinkler lines are aluminum pipes and are about twenty feet long with a three-foot sprinkler head on each one of them. The pipes come in two different sizes: four-inch pipe and six-inch pipe. Roy and I were lucky enough to have the task of moving four-inch pipelines. Each pipe had a connector that would fit into the previous pipe. The only way to connect the pipes together was to violently shove one pipe into the other pipe, connecting the two. The sprinkler pipes were about sixty feet apart from each other and ran down the field about a quarter of a mile. When all the pipes were joined at the end of the field, we would insert an end plug and turn on the water at the opposite end. The pipes would fill, and the water pressure would cause the sprinkler heads to turn, thus spewing water in about a twenty-foot radius.

What does this have to do with Uncle Gene? As legend would have it, Uncle Gene would turn on the water first before he would start laying the sprinkler lines. Attempting a feat like that would never cross the minds of people like Roy and I and any other field laborers. Uncle Gene was not an average field laborer. Not only would he turn the water on first but he would also move two sections of six-inch pipe at the same time. This was not an easy task. By the time he joined all the pipes together at the opposite end of the field, the water would constantly rise. As he joined the last section of pipe, he would insert the end plug, and the sprinklers would work perfectly. This method would save time as he would not have to walk the entire length of the field to turn the water on.

Uncle Gene eventually landed a job as a union laborer. He worked for a general contractor named Terry Mooreland, who was also a teacher at Delano High School. Mr. Mooreland drove a Rolls-Royce, and Uncle Gene was impressed by his boss's success. Uncle Gene also knew the difference between owning a business and working for someone else. Although he was not educated in school, he was a free-spirited businessman. He began to buy old houses in his neighborhood and fixed them up for rentals. By doing this, he always had cash flow and never needed to borrow money from anyone. As far as I am concerned, he was financially successful.

Another thing that impressed me about Uncle Gene was that he was a devoted family man. Like I mentioned before, he married my aunt Honey, who was previously married to my dad's oldest brother, Uncle Booney. He worked very hard to keep the family unit together, and all the kids respected him for that. He was devoted to Aunt Honey even when she suffered from diabetes in the latter years of her life. She eventually lost both of her legs, and he cared for her until she died.

I had a very good relationship with Uncle Gene because he was impressed by how smart I was by spelling the word *hippopotamus*. Since spelling words was my best subject at school and being a little bit of a show-off, I quickly took the stage in front of about ten of my relatives to show them my newly discovered talent. I started to sound off each letter, "H-I-P-P-O-P-O-T-A-M-A-U-S." After I finished, there was a great applause and a few "Oohs" and "Aahs." I did my best Flip Wilson and stuck my little chest out with great pride as I soaked up all of the audiences' attention.

After this incredible event ended, I realized that I had misspelled the word. Apparently, no one else there knew how to spell *hippopotamus* either, so I was not corrected. There was no way I was going to go back and make that correction since I was the star of the show. After spelling (or misspelling) that word, according to Uncle Gene, I was the smartest boy on the planet. He would continuously brag to everyone for the rest of his life how incredibly intelligent I was. Boy, if he only knew the truth. If this incident would have happened in Kim's family (my future wife), someone would have sniffed me out immediately and would have asked me how to spell G-O-A-T.

AUNT BESSIE

Aunt Bessie was one of Mama's many sisters. She was a little older than Mama, and she lived in Bakersfield on the infamous Cottonwood Road. She had a few children that were close to our ages, so we always had someone to play with that was within our respective age groups. She had married a man whose last name was Turner. I remember never seeing him there at the house. In fact, none of us kids had never met him. We were too young to understand separation or divorce back then, especially when it did not occur too often. I found out later in life that they were separated because both Aunt Bessie and her husband suffered from mental illness and they could not properly take care of their children.

Aunt Bessie was living alone with her five children in the early 1960s. Apparently, at this particular time, she was able to care for her children with the aid of California's welfare system. Her kids' names were Joann, Maryann, Butch, Bikey, and Cookie. Aunt Bessie and her family lived near Uncle Gene and Aunt Honey's house, so we would sometimes visit both families on the same trip. We would do all the fun stuff that kids would do back in those days, like playing hide-and-seek and tag. There were a few times that Aunt Bessie would come up to the South Ranch along with her kids. Like all of our cousins who visited the South Ranch, they loved being out in the country.

All of a sudden, in the mid—to late-1960s, we didn't see Aunt Bessie and our cousins anymore. I really didn't understand where they had gone. In the early 1970s, Aunt Bessie resurfaced. She was living in Central Bakersfield and was married to a man by the name of Aaron McCowan. She had a daughter named Rosetta (Rosie) who was about two years younger than Lulu. Mama would take me, Baylo, and Lulu to visit Aunt Bessie and her new family at times. There was another girl living with them that was about six years older than we were. Her name was Marilyn, and I remember Aunt Bessie constantly calling out her name, "Marilyn, Marilyn, come here." I would sometimes feel a little sorry for Marilyn because she seemed to be at Aunt Bessie's beckon call. Looking back, I think that Marilyn must have been Aaron's daughter from a previous marriage. Also, I would later find out that Aunt Bessie's children from her first marriage would be sent to foster care. In my mid-thirties, I would meet my cousin (one of Aunt Bessie's daughters) who was living in Sacramento who would tell me the entire story of what really happened. More on that in a later chapter.

BERT FROM ALLENSWORTH

Mama, who has always been quite outgoing, had friends all over the place. She seemed to know just about everyone. As I mentioned earlier, there was a small town west of Earlimart called Allensworth. Mama had an African American friend in Allensworth named Martha Pope who had a few kids. She would take me with her sometimes because Martha had a boy named Bert that was about the same age as I was. Bert also had an older sister and a brother named Mark, who was about the same age as Terry.

I was probably about seven or eight years old when I first met Bert. We would go to their house, and Mama would visit Martha while Bert and I played Monopoly in his bedroom. This was the very first time that I had played that legendary game. He had a few toys that were pretty cool as well, so I always looked forward to visiting him. Bert was a very gregarious little boy with a natural gift of gab. He always had me laughing because he was, well, just funny. Some people just naturally have the type of personality that attracts others. Bert was the kind of person that probably didn't have an enemy in the world. Life just always seemed to be one big party for him. I always loved being around him.

Unfortunately, Bert was attending grade school in Allensworth, so I would only see him on an occasional visit. Bert and his family would eventually move to Earlimart (the barrio) during our junior high school years, so I would see him more often. Bert will be mentioned in later chapters since he was a part of my childhood. I have some fun stories about him that you will really enjoy. So stay tuned.

THE DEVIL MADE ME DO IT!

The late great comedian Flip Wilson had a famous saying. He would always say, "The devil made me do it." That simple quote became famous among many Americans during the late 1960s and early 1970s. It made sense because, even at a very young age, I knew right from wrong. I believe that most people of sound mind do as well. However, as humans, we sometimes make bad choices even if we know that certain consequences might not be in our favor.

When we were kids growing up at the South Ranch, we would love to watch cartoons on Saturday mornings. One of our favorite ones was the *Flintstones*. I bring this up because there was one episode when Fred has two imaginary characters on his shoulders. I believe that he was on a diet and got up in the middle of the night and went to the refrigerator. He knew that he was not supposed to eat a late-night snack. One of the characters was an angel, and the other one was a devil. Fred was faced with a difficult decision and didn't know what he should do.

The little angel who looked like Fred and had a halo over his head told him to not eat that "Brontosaurus Burger." However, the little devil, who also looked like Fred with a red face, horns, and a menacing smile, told Fred to eat that delicious snack and to forget what his counterpart (the angel) was saying and to take care of his rumbling stomach. Now, I said all that to say this. There is a lot of truth to that episode of the *Flintstones* because we humans are constantly being summoned by these two characters of the mind. All I can say is choose wisely.

B. HOWARD'S HORSES

In the summer of 1969, Mama took me and Terry to visit Mama Tina and Daddy Wright. It was just like the usual visit in which we would say hello to our grandparents and then head straight for Daddy Wright's candy drawer. He always had several pieces of candy waiting for us. Way to go, Daddy Wright. Anyway, after we got our special treats, we would go outside to play with whomever we would see. On this particular day, we saw Arroyo Brown riding his bike at the south end of Oak Street. Arroyo, who was Soot's (his mother's) one and only boy, always had plenty of toys, including a big wheel, so Terry and I would always go around the corner to play at his house.

Directly across the street from Arroyo's house was an open pasture that was fenced in. It was about two acres of land that a guy by the name of B. Howard owned. B. Howard probably owned about forty acres in all. Most of his land was covered by grape vineyards in which he would turn into raisins. He also lived on his land in a fairly decent home that was surrounded by a lot of trees. B. Howard was kind of a recluse and basically minded his own business. He also owned a few horses that would roam in his pasture.

On that particular day, I guess that Terry, Arroyo, and I must have been bored because the idea that we came up with was not that bright. One of our favorite pastimes was throwing dirt clods (rocks) at each other. On many occasions, we would team up with other kids in the barrio (usually two per team) and have these rock fights. Terry and I got very good at throwing rocks. Not only were we accurate but we could also throw for long distances.

Terry could always throw farther than I could because like I said earlier, he was exactly four-and-a-half years older than I was. However, I would not let the age difference deter me. I would have a rock-throwing contest whenever he challenged me. Constantly throwing rocks (especially at the South Ranch) was a way of life back then. Throwing rocks at a young age would eventually serve me well a few years later when playing baseball. Even at my current age (fifty-eight) I still have a very good arm. I am known as a world-class "rock skipper" among my friends in the Bay Area that have seen me throw rocks during camping trips.

WORKING OVERTIME AND SETTING THE STAGE

We have a saying in the African American community that states, "The devil is always busy." However, on that day, he must have been working overtime. I am sure that he noticed three little boys that were bored and some horses in a nearby field. In one of my favorite movies, *The Devil's Advocate*, Al Pacino, who plays the devil, said that he does not make decisions for people. His job was only to set the stage and let us make our own decisions. With that being said, all I can say is that the devil was a "stage-setting motherf#cka" on that day.

With no angels and no halos in sight, he stood all alone on the shoulders of me, Terry, and Arroyo that afternoon. Knowing that we were bored and that we were expert rock throwers, he convinced us to do the unthinkable. With the skills of a maestro, he carefully orchestrated his evil deeds. Before we knew it, we were climbing the wire fence to enter the horses' domain. After we all got inside, we noticed that there were four adult (big) horses near the center of the pasture. They were casually grazing the lush grass and not noticing a thing. As we got closer to them, one horse lifted his head up and seemed to get a little nervous. With Terry leading the way, Arroyo and I watched as Terry got closer. It was not until later in life that we would learn to never approach a horse from the rear. Since he was definitely in charge, I guess that the devil didn't give a fat rat's a#s about that "never approach a horse from the rear" sh#t.

With rocks in our hands and extra ones stuffed in our pockets, we ambushed [laugh] the poor creatures, or so we thought. Terry got directly behind one of the horses, which was a beautiful Appaloosa, and threw his rock as hard as he could directly at the horse's booty. We heard a loud *thud* as the horse immediately kicked both of his legs up into the air, narrowly missing Terry. You would think that after that narrow miss, we would have learned our lesson and realized that we were playing with dangerous animals that were at least one thousand pounds each. But the devil was not having it. Not on that day. Unbeknownst to us, he cleverly set the stage again and had all the horses go into a corner. This was easy pickin's for three little rambunctious boys, or so we thought.

As the horses got into the corner, all four of them were facing away from us with their rear ends pointed toward us. Terry was on point again as we got within about five feet of the horses. Knowing what was coming next, one of the horses beat Terry to the punch and kicked his left leg back. His hoof hit Terry squarely on his knee. Terry immediately grabbed his knee and fell to the ground. Within a second, he was up and running with me and Arroyo heading to the nearest exit. We all jumped over the fence in a hurry, realizing how stupid we had been. Terry's knee was not too bad. Luckily, it was just a small bruise.

We got safely over the fence and seemingly out of harm's way, but the devil was not finished setting his stage. In fact, he had an encore performance that was so good (not) it still gives me chills sometimes when I think about it. He had somehow coerced the single worst possible person to show up and witness our little adventure. Of course that person was—you guessed it—Daddy. Houston, we got a problem.

As Terry, Arroyo, and I got back into what most people would consider "safe territory" (away from the horses), Terry and I knew that being back in that pasture with those dangerous horses was definitely a safer place than being on Oak Street with Daddy. Arroyo Brown (lucky little negro) escaped Daddy because he was not part of our family. I wish that I could say the same for me and Terry. As Daddy sat in his blue 1968 Chevy Impala, he gestured for us to come to him. Arroyo Brown was safely back at his house by then. Daddy, who was wearing one of his dress hats because it was Sunday, demanded that we meet him at Aunt Plute's house. Somehow that little hat made him look all the more menacing.

As we walked slowly toward Aunt Plute's front gate, Daddy was parking his car in the driveway. He abruptly got out of his car and told us, "What the h#ll were you guys doing out in B. Howard's pasture?" Of course he knew the answer, but I guess hearing it directly from the "horse's mouth" (pun intended, low-hanging fruit) would be part of our punishment. Terry and I could do nothing but shrug our shoulders and have a look of innocence that we hoped would help us in some way. But deep down, we knew that our as#es were grass and he was the lawn mower.

Daddy knocked loudly on Aunt Plute's front door, and she immediately let us in. He asked her if could borrow her bedroom. Aunt Plute said yes as she looked at me and Terry with empathy. She knew in her heart that she could not deter Daddy from what was about to take place. All I can say is that it was not good for two "devilish" little boys.

WHOOPIN' BOYS

I want to spend a little time talking about "whoopins." Some people would call them *whippings*, which I guess is the proper pronunciation. Since my family was from the South and we were black, they were called whoopins. Whatever the case, all I knew was that they were very unpleasant and, to be honest, a child's worst nightmare. I want to make it clear that we were living in different times back then and getting whoopins was not unusual. I would also like to say that I never looked at Mama and Daddy any different when we received our punishments. I believed our whoopins were warranted 99.9 percent of the time.

One thing that I didn't believe was that bullsh#t line when people (usually parents) would say that "This whoopin' is going to hurt me way more than it hurts you." Whoever came up with that saying must have never been at the wrong end of a belt. However, there was only one time in which I thought that Terry and I didn't deserve a whoopin'. I'll get into that a little later. So with that said, let's "whoop it up."

I will try to explain whoopins in the best way that I can since there are different kinds of whoopins. In the hood, the word *whoopin(s)* can be used in many contexts such as an "a#s whoopin" or "I'm gonna whoop yo a#s." The former can be used in the same way as being spanked as a way of punishment. The latter can be used as a threat to physically assault someone. I will be talking about the differences in the former because we had two different people administering the punishments. Those people were no other than Mama and Daddy.

MAMA, MAY I? NO, YOU MAY NOT

Mama had a very unique way of administering punishment to us kids. I can hardly remember her hitting any of the other kids, only me and Terry. This might just be a mental block of mine, but I am being serious. For some reason, in my mind, Terry and I were the true "whoopin' boys" of the family. I remember Mama yelling at us to stop doing whatever "mannish" little thing we were doing. When we didn't respond, she would pick up anything in her reach—a belt, a shoe, and God forbid, the kitchen sink—that was available to inflict pain on us. She would also tell us to do the unimaginable and pick a limb (switch) from one of the trees and bring it back to her so she could whoop us. Pure psychological torture, right? However, her first weapon of choice was her hand. She had a forehand and a back hand that would make Serena Williams proud. She would draw her arm all the way back to the Louisiana swamplands and hit us with pinpoint accuracy.

I remember her taking me and Terry to Bakersfield to shop at Montgomery Ward for school clothes. Terry and I had made some money by working in the grape fields that summer. She stayed in the car but reminded us to not ride on the escalators because she thought that they could be dangerous for kids. Escalators were kind of a new thing back then, so we were definitely intrigued by them. We promised her that we would not ride them of course. As we entered that huge department store, the first thing that caught our eyes were, of course, those escalators. When I enter a store today, I don't even notice the escalators. They are simply just a tool that is used to get from one floor to another. However, when you were a kid back in those days, an escalator was equivalent to one of the best rides that you would see at Six Flags today.

After buying our school clothes, Terry and I had a decision to make. We could happily walk out of the store and avoid any potential conflict with Mama, or we could take a chance and ride the escalators hoping that she had forgotten her prior warning. Somehow we convinced ourselves that riding the escalators "just once" would be okay and that we would not be disobeying Mama. So we rode the escalators up to the second floor and back down to the main floor. Looking back now, I realize that that quick ride of true bliss was not worth the punishment that we were about to receive.

When we got back to the car, the FIRST thing that Mama asked us was, Did we ride those escalators? Our initial response of silence along with our telltale roaming eyes, convinced her that we had indeed ridden those dangerous machines. As we sat in the back seat of the car, she reminded us how she had told us not to ride those escalators. Then, with a sudden flurry and amazing skill, she reached back and started to hit me and Terry with her open hand. We held our arms up to help us from the onslaught; however, some of the blows got through to our shoulders and backs. Mama would never intentionally hit us in the face or any other vital areas. So we always knew that if we could live through the initial outburst, we would be okay; and indeed we were. There was definitely an "added cost" to the clothes that we purchased that day. That added cost was the cost of an a#s whoopin'.

Since we are on the subject of whoopins, I would like to share another story that I will never forget. I remember one Saturday morning in the summer of 1968 in which I again deliberately disobeyed Mama. It started off as a typical Saturday morning with most of us kids watching cartoons on the television. I decided to venture outside to play in the yard. To my surprise, a little black-and-white dog suddenly appeared out of nowhere. This was not that uncommon since many dogs were taken out to the country from nearby towns and abandoned. Like most kids, I immediately liked the friendly little dog. While I was petting the little canine, Mama, who was inside the house, came to the front screen door and told me to not feed that dog and to leave him alone. She was hoping that he would eventually leave the South Ranch and find somewhere else to live.

After saying that, Mama went back into the house and went about her business. I, however, had other plans. When the coast was clear, I went to the back entrance of the house and sneaked into the kitchen and grabbed a chicken bone from the previous night's meal. The little dog scarfed it down immediately and started to wag its tail. An immediate friendship was started as he started to lick me as I petted him incessantly.

A true bonding of a country boy and his dog is never cemented until we go on a hunting trip. I immediately headed due west through the cotton field, which was about knee-high by then, to get to the grape field, where jackrabbit hunting was much better because of the open space. By the time I got to the grape field, which was one quarter of a mile away, a small figure came into my peripheral vision. Although I had 20/20 vision back then, I still couldn't recognize who it was. As the little dog and I stood there, I was finally able to make out who the person was. It was Mama. I still didn't immediately think anything out of the ordinary until she got closer. As she got about halfway down the cotton field, I again realized that it was Mama. But this was no ordinary Mama. This was Mama walking with her head down and a switch in her right hand.

Immediately I went into panic mode when I saw the switch because, all of a sudden, my mind replayed everything that she told me not to do. I knew that I was in big trouble. As she got closer, she gestured to me to come to her. As I started to walk due east through the cotton field to meet her, I could feel the impending doom within my bones. I knew that I had f#cked up! As we met up with each other, the first thing that she said was "I told you not to feed that dog and to leave him alone, didn't I?"

I said yes as my voice cracked and my eyes started to water. Then, with amazing speed, she grabbed my left arm and held on tightly. I started to jump up and down as she started to whoop me with the switch that was still in her right hand. As I continued to struggle and dance around like I was doing something between the Funky Chicken, the Twist, and the Worm, she finally stopped. As the tears ran down my eyes, I realized that I had learned a valuable lesson: don't disobey Mama. Your very life could depend on it.

STOP PLAYING UNDER YOUR CLOTHES

One thing that I want you to know about Mama is that she is a devout Christian woman who grew up in the South. She lived by the words of the Bible and was determined to have her kids follow suit. We would attend church and Sunday School on occasion in Teviston at Reverend Daniel's church. I am sure we would have gone to church more regularly if Mama had not been battling her mental illness throughout our childhoods. She came from a family that would attend church several times a week. I know some of you readers can relate, right? Mama had certain rules that her kids had to abide by. Obedience was the first one that comes to mind. She would always say that "A disobedient child will not live their days out." Another rule that comes to mind is no cussing, especially cussing with the name "God" in it. "Don't use the Lord's name in vain," she would often say, especially to Daddy, who, by the way, was not on the "no cussing" bandwagon.

Another thing I remember her telling me was to "stop playing under my clothes." I could not understand why something like having my hand on my penis was such a bad thing, especially since it felt kinda good. What can I say, I liked playing with my d#ck. However, as I got older and started to learn more about life and the way that many Southern Baptists thought about sex back then, I could see why Mama would say something like that. Sex was considered a "dirty act" to the people who raised her. Masturbation was considered a mortal sin by both my parents, so anything along those lines was taboo. Now, I could understand why Mama told me to get my hand out of my pants. It's not a polite thing to do in public.

However, being the innovative kid that I was, I learned to hide my devious little act. Instead of outwardly putting my hand directly down my pants, I would instead put my hand in my pocket, where (as far as Mama was concerned) I kept small toys like marbles and so on. Through pure innovation and a desire to explore, I discovered what many young boys also discovered at that age, and that was "pocket pool." As I got into my teen years, I would hear kids joking, saying things like "If you masturbate, you will go blind or you will grow hair in your palm." My reply to that? "I guess that I'm gonna be a blind hairy-palmed motherf#ka!" One last thing. The late great Redd Foxx once said, "When I was a kid, we was so po that the only thing that I had to play with was my d#ck!" Enough said.

JUDGE DADDY

You've heard of Judge Judy, right? Well, in our family, we had another person in a similar role. The other person that was in the "whoopin' business" was Daddy. In fact, I would refer to him as the chief, founder, CEO, president, or any other word that would describe an experienced person that was a master at their craft. Also, you could call him the judge, jury, and the executioner. In fact, Daddy was so good at it that he created an experience in which he would never even have to whoop us. When we kids (mostly me and Terry) got out of line, all Daddy would have to do was to reach for his belt as if he were going to draw his weapon of mass destruction, only to have us immediately straighten up. This was very effective for him and definitely effective for saving our little hides. His style was definitely different from Mama's.

Now, I don't want this to sound like Daddy was abusive to us. He was definitely not. Also, we didn't get whooped all the time. There were just a few times in our lives that we got "taken out to the woodshed." The B. Howard fiasco was one of the more memorable times that I can remember getting whooped. Trust me, I am not saying "memorable" in a feel-good nostalgic way. I am saying it in a "I wish that I could forget it but can't" kind of way.

After getting to Aunt Plute's house after getting in trouble for throwing rocks at those horses, Daddy took Terry into Aunt Plute's bedroom first. All I could hear was the sound of a belt swishing through the air, some rumbling noises from Terry's attempted escape, some loud "licks" from the belt reaching its target, and Terry's loud screams.

Needless to say, I was terrified. After about ten seconds of pure hell for Terry, he was let out of the bedroom. His eyes were watering as he hastily walked past me. Then, it was my turn. I was already crying before Daddy even laid a hand on me. I was hoping that he would have some pity on me if he saw me crying. I was wrong. He closed the door and gave me the same treatment as he gave Terry. Although it only lasted about ten seconds as well, it seemed like an eternity. We both had a few whip marks on our arms, legs, and backs. I guess we learned our lesson because we never went into B. Howard's pasture again. Neither did the devil.

Ain't Misbehavin'

The only time that I thought that we didn't deserve a whoopin was a time when Terry and I were getting a haircut at Po'Boy's. For some reason, Terry and I had a bad case of the giggles that day. We were always constantly teasing each other like most brothers do. However, we didn't stop even when we were getting a haircut. As I sat in Po'Boy's barber chair, Terry would make funny faces that would make me laugh. Of course, laughing hysterically would make my head move, and Po'Boy couldn't cut my hair properly. Daddy had gone to the local store to pick something up, so me and Terry were alone at Po'Boy's. I could tell that Po'Boy was getting annoyed by palming the top of my head to keep it in place. Somehow he made it through and was still able to give me a pretty good haircut.

When Terry got in the chair, I showed no remorse and made the funniest monkey face that I could. Of course, Terry couldn't maintain his composure and started to laugh out loud as well. Po'Boy still didn't say one word, although he still looked irritated. As he finished cutting Terry's hair, Daddy arrived back on the scene. As all three of us headed back for the car, Po'Boy motioned Daddy to come back inside. After waiting in the car for about five minutes, Daddy, who had a mad look on his face, told us that Po'Boy told him how bad we were acting. Daddy said that we embarrassed him and that he was going to give us a whoopin' when we got home. I must say that this trip back to the South Ranch after getting a haircut was not nearly as fun as the other ones. After getting home and receiving our punishment, Terry and I often wondered if that whoopin' was necessary. I sometimes still wonder about that today. What do you think?

THE FAMILY AROUND
THE CORNER

There was another African American family that lived near 1008 Oak Street. Larvell "Soot" Owens was a half black, half Native American woman who was from Tucson, Arizona. She was the salt of the earth, was very gregarious, and loved everybody. She was "high yella" in complexion and short and sturdy in stature. She had three kids that were close to my age. The oldest, Marlinda Owens, was dark skinned, skinny, and had a similar personality to her mother's. She was the same age as Baylo. Fransette "Sissy" Owens, who was also "high yella," was her second daughter who was kind of quiet and reserved. She was naturally a little robust, the direct opposite of Marlinda. She was about one year older than I was. Then there was Arroyo Brown whose father was part African American and part Filipino. Arroyo was Lulu's age. Lulu, Baylo, Terry, and I would go over and visit from time to time when we were in town. Baylo would play with Marlinda and Sissy. Lulu and I and sometimes Terry would hang out with Arroyo at different times. The good thing about the family around the corner is that they all had bicycles. They had no problem sharing them with the "country folk" (us). However, Arroyo was a little reluctant in sharing his bike most of the time, but he would allow Terry to be his driver and give him rides.

Lulu, Baylo, and I would take turns riding Marlinda's and Sissy's bikes up and down Oak Street. We would have such a great time because we didn't have any bikes at the South Ranch. Every now and then, we would fall off the bikes and skin our knees like most kids do, but that did not stop us from riding all over Earlimart. One time when we were gone on a bike ride, we found out that Marlinda had been taken to the hospital in Delano. Apparently, she had something called asthma in which her breathing became impaired. When we got back, Sissy explained to us that she sometimes would have these asthma attacks. It scared us a little, but before too long, she was back at home and we were playing together again.

LOVERBOY NEO

One day in 1970 when I was by myself visiting our kinfolk at 1008 Oak Street, I wandered around the corner to visit Arroyo. Apparently, he and Soot had gone to Delano on an errand. When I knocked on the door, Sissy answered. She told me that Arroyo and her mother were gone and that they would be back later. She offered me to come in and have some Kool-Aid that she had just made. Of course I said yes. Even at that young age, a country boy loved him some Kool-Aid! I noticed that that Marlinda was also there and that they were playing the game of Monopoly on the living room floor. They asked if I wanted to play and of course I said, yes. I had previously played Monopoly at Bert's house in Allensworth, so I knew that it was a fun game. What I didn't know, however, was that Marlinda and Sissy had a different version of the game that me and Bert used to play. Now, the game of Monopoly itself, with all the little trinkets, the board, and all the fake money, were exactly the same as the one at Bert's house. However, there were two very different elements of this Monopoly game that were entirely different from the previous games in which I had played. And their names were Marlinda and Sissy.

They played a version of Monopoly that I had never seen before. Now, I know what you are thinking and that was not the case, well, sort of. If Marlinda and Sissy's version of Monopoly had been a movie, it would have been rated PG-13 (approximately their ages at the time) I guess. Sorry, more low-hanging fruit. I couldn't help myself. Anyway, the rule was if I lost the game, I would be kissed by the two of them. Now, these rules would have sounded good to most heterosexual teenage boys; but I was only a kid, so the rules made me a little nervous but not nervous enough to leave. Let's just put it this way, I was a lot more curious than I was nervous. As the game proceeded for about an hour, I realized that I was not going to win, even though I was in second place. I would have to beat both of them to win. My odds were not good.

Marlinda finally won the game, and it was time to pay up. With a great show of affection, they both kissed me numerous times on my cheeks. I would like to say that they kissed me on the lips (so I could go brag to my friends), but they didn't. After the kissing session and my last drink of Kool-Aid, I headed for the front door. I walked back around the corner to 1008 Oak Street with a little smile on my face. After that day, we never played Monopoly under those circumstances again. Marlinda and Sissy, as well as I, never mentioned that day again. Like Scar said to Simba in the animated version of *The Lion King*, "It's our little secret."

FIREWORKS AT THE SOUTH RANCH

Every Fourth of July was a very fun time at the South Ranch. Mama would take us to Delano and buy some fireworks at the fireworks stand. We didn't have much money, but we had a few dollars from working in the fields in the summertime. When nighttime came, all of us kids would sit out in the dirt driveway on lawn chairs and watch the fireworks show that was about four miles away in Delano. I still remember vividly the bright and colorful fireworks that were a joy to watch. I remember the "oohs" and "aahs" from our whole family. After the fireworks show in Delano ended, we had our own firework show. I still have warm feelings of nostalgia every time I think of those warm summer nights in July at the South Ranch. It was such a blessing to have all our family there sharing memories that would last forever. Some of our best memories were truly "born on the Fourth of July."

Food at the South Ranch

Eating at the South Ranch was always an adventure. If you can imagine one "mama bird' doling out food to seven hungry little vultures, then you might know what I am getting at. Mama cooked all the meals, which were primarily in the evenings. We kids would fend for ourselves for breakfast and lunch. Breakfast would usually consist of some kind of cereal, like Fruit Loops, Cheerios, and my two favorites, Cap'n Crunch and Coco Crispies. I loved (and still do) the way that cereal made the milk turn chocolate. We would also have hot cereal like cream of wheat, oatmeal, and my favorite hot cereal, Malt-O-Meal. Terry and I were the only kids that liked hot cereal, so we were able to feast alone in the great Serengeti (our living room) without being bothered by jackals and other scavengers.

We all learned how to cook the basics, like bacon and eggs, at a very young age. Trust me, learning how to cook the basics was a means of survival back then. Mama didn't cook breakfast and lunch, so we didn't have a formal mealtime other than dinner. We ate snacks and junk food whenever Mama had to go to the store to get groceries. Mama was very nice about letting us go to the supermarket in Pixley once a week (usually on Saturday) after Daddy got his paycheck. Most of us would pile into the car and make the trip; however, sometimes some of us would stay at the South Ranch and place an order. Placing an order would mean that one of us kids would bring the person that stayed at home some sweet snacks. Our favorite combination was a cupcake and an ice cream. Dolly Madison had Zingers and other delicious mouth-watering treats that were to die for. They also had some great ice cream bars, like a sidewalk sundae, banana split, and a Long John.

Eating sweets was a popular thing at the South Ranch. Sometimes Mama and Daddy would surprise us with some "thousand cookies." We called them thousand cookies (cream filled) because of the amount of cookies that were in the package. The manufacturers sure knew what they were doing when making those cookies. Kudos to their marketing department because they were cheap and there were enough cookies to feed our whole family of little hyenas.

CORNBREAD ALL IN MY HAIR

Since Mama only cooked dinner, she would prepare the meal in advance. Not being the richest family in the area and on a tight budget, Mama had to get very creative with meals that would feed all of us. And creative she was. She got really good at cooking one of the greatest types of gourmet food that was ever created—beans. That's right, beans. She would start cooking them in the mid-afternoon, and by dinner time, they would be ready. She would cook lima beans, pinto beans, butter beans, and on occasion and to our delight, chili beans. She would also cook some fried chicken along with the beans sometimes. We used to have a pecking order (here I go again) with the chicken parts. As soon as we knew that we were having chicken, all of us kids would yell out what piece we wanted. "I want a leg," "I want the back," "I want the thigh," "I want the neck," and "I want the liver and the gizzard," we would yell, knowing that that was the only guarantee that you were going to get what you wanted. It's interesting how we kids abided by the code of "first come, first serve." As long as you called it out, there were never any problems. Sometimes Mama would make some cornbread to go along with the chili beans and the fried chicken. This was definitely a special treat. In the African American culture, we have a saying when a person is really enjoying a great meal. We call it "greasin'." Anyway, there was one time that I was enjoying that special meal so much that I had grease on my cheeks and cornbread in my hair. I was truly "greasin'."

Daddy Knows "Breast"

Daddy, who was considered the man of the house, would not have to be involved in our silly little game of calling out for chicken parts. Apparently, by birthright, he inherited the best part of the chicken. Of course I am being facetious, but it sure seemed that way. Whenever we started to call out our pieces, we knew better not to even mention the most scrumptious, delectable, and satisfying part of the chicken. That, of course, was the breast. Since he worked all day long in the fields doing mostly manual labor, Daddy believed he deserved the best part of the chicken. We kids never argued about it or anything. It was just the way it was. Looking back now, I think we kids appreciated Daddy working all the time and figured that he did deserve the chicken breast. Sometimes Daddy would not eat all his chicken breast and would leave some of that tender white meat on the bone. When that happened, all I can say is it was like "ducks on a junebug."

HOLIDAY MEALS

The best time for eating was on holidays like Thanksgiving, Christmas, and Easter. Mama would cook a turkey and dressing along with some greens with ham hocks. She would also bake some cakes and make my favorite dessert, which was sweet potato pie. Now, I am starting to wonder when the next holiday is because writing about all this food is making a brotha hungry. The best part about the holidays was that we would do something called triple dippin'. I am sure you have heard of double dippin', right? Well, on holidays, we would eat Mama's food in the morning, since she usually stayed up all night preparing it. Instead of letting it sit all day, we just figured that we would not hurt Mama's feelings and would start on the food as soon as she finished it. It was a hard job, but someone had to do it. Plus, it's what good little vultures should do anyway, right?

After practically devouring all the food at the South Ranch for breakfast, we would all pile into the car and go to 1008 Oak Street for lunch. That's right, lunch. Even though it might be around 10:30 a.m. or 11:00 a.m., we figured that was close enough to lunch time. Back in those days, we didn't have brunch. Plus, if brunch was invented by then, I am pretty sure that it was for rich white people, not for us hungry heathens. Anyway, since Aunt Plute's house was in the front of the lot, we figured we would pay her and her family a visit. Aunt Plute was a master at cooking a glazed ham, a hen and dressing, greens, cornbread, and fantastic desserts like carrot cakes, sweet potato pies, and her specialty, apple pie.

She always had her food ready early in the day as well; so on semi-full stomachs, we ate for the second time. The flavor of Aunt's Plute's food was different from Mama's, but it was all good! After stuffing our little bellies like hungry lion cubs, we went outside to play for a while. After running around and playing for about two hours, guess what happened? We were hungry again. That's right, hungry again. I still don't know today how we would be hungry after eating two big meals that close together. But nevertheless, we were indeed hungry again. This time we had our sights and our bellies set on Mama Tina and Daddy Wright's house. We knew that Mama Tina always cooked on holidays as well. She would also have all the goodies that Mama and Aunt Plute would cook, like a hen and dressing, pies and cakes, and my very favorite, banana pudding. We would stuff our little gourds to the max again. By this time it was late afternoon, so I guess we could call it dinner. By the time the day ended, we all got back into the car and headed back to the South Ranch where, you guessed it, we had Mama's leftovers.

COMMODESIE FOOD

There were times at the South Ranch where Daddy's paycheck wasn't quite enough to feed all of us kids. Mama and Daddy signed up for a program called (for you young readers who may not have heard of it) welfare. Welfare back then was a program that helped families "bridge the gap" by giving out monthly checks and giving out food. I remember Mama driving to Earlimart to pick up the welfare food. I don't remember any of us kids ever going along for the ride. I just remember her unloading some packaged food that she called commodesie food. Looking back, I am sure that she meant to say "Commodity food." But at the time, as hungry as I was, all I cared about was the most important part of that name, which was no other than the word *food*.

Even as a kid, I must say that the welfare food was not that appealing. Powdered milk (yuck!), canned meat (okay), and raisins (good) were the things that I remembered most. No one ever drank the powdered milk. Unbeknownst to Mama or Daddy, the canned meat (similar to Spam but not as good) was sometimes given to the dogs by me. I am sure that I would have gotten a whoopin' if I got caught. Of course the canned meat was a gourmet meal for our dogs, who usually got kitchen scraps. They would definitely "wolf it down." Mama, who had a really good sense of humor, would tell us about her favorite meal when she was a child growing up in Louisiana in a family of sixteen children. She said that when food was scarce, the would have "poke and grits". Now, that didn't sound bad at all to me. In fact, it sounded kind of good. But when she told us what it really consisted of, all we could do was laugh. She said when you have poke and grits, it really means you poke out your mouth and grit your teeth because there was no food at all. Fortunately, poke and grits was not on the menu at the South Ranch. Thank God.

THE WORKERS AT THE SOUTH RANCH

The South Ranch was sometimes a bustling place especially early in the mornings. During certain times of the year (planting season and harvesting season), there would be a lot of workers around. Vignolo Farms was a fast-growing business. He had acres upon acres spread out in the South Central Valley. The eighty-acre South Ranch was just a drop in the bucket within all the other ranches that he owned. Just in our area, there were a few other ranches with vast acreage. There was the North Ranch, Del Mart, the West Ranch, the East Ranch, and Kimberlina Road Ranch, just to name a few.

Vignolo had countless employees managing and operating these ranches. They were growers, packers, and shippers. Daddy was considered a farm laborer, which meant that he did just about anything that needed to be done. Looking back, I can see what a skilled worker Daddy was. He was an operator of many types of heavy equipment, including bulldozers and wheeled tractors. He also was skilled at irrigation, which was a huge responsibility. Watering the crops correctly was critical to the yields during harvest time. He was also a skilled mechanic, which means he sometimes worked on various farming equipment. He was definitely a pro, and he took great pride in his work.

The workers that I remember most were some of the ones that worked at the South Ranch consistently.

Manuel Gutierrez

Manuel Gutierrez was in charge of the irrigation process at the South Ranch. He was pretty short (about five feet, four inches) with a balding head. He had a family that was living at the North Ranch, which was about three miles north of the South Ranch. He had about nine or ten children in which some of them we knew pretty well. They were various ages with some of them being exactly our age. There was Percy, Johnny, Alfred, George, Sonia, and Adam, just to name a few. Manuel had a great personality and would always joke around with me and Terry.

There was one incident that he witnessed that he would never let me live down. Apparently, when I was getting that infamous whoopin' by Mama that day in the field, he was sitting in his truck about one hundred yards away. He told me he had seen the whole thing. For him, it was considered "prime theater" at a place (the South Ranch) that was usually kind of boring for him. He watched closely as I got my little booty whooped. He thought that it was the funniest thing that he had ever seen. Truth be known, I didn't think it was funny worth a "g#d d#mn." So for the next few years, every time that he saw me, which was a lot, he would remind me of that whoopin'. He would work himself into a frenzy of laughter, mimicking my every move as I tried desperately to get out of Mama's grip. He thought that it was the funniest thing that he ever saw. I thought it was about as funny as a train wreck.

Al "Good Kid" Stewart

Al Stewart was a dark-skinned African American man that had been working with Vignolo Farms since its inception. He was nicknamed Good Kid because Al was everybody's friend. He was also a skilled worker that taught Daddy many facets about working on a farm. Daddy used to tell me that whenever he was assigned to work the day with Al, he knew it was going to be a good day. Al, who was originally from the South, would constantly tell Daddy some of those old Southern dirty jokes. He would have Daddy in stitches all day long.

Whenever we would see Al, he would wave his right hand and say, "What do you bet?" Then he would smile from ear to ear (flashing his grill way before it became popular among rappers) and let out a big laugh. Al lived in a small house that looked like a cabin that was just south of town outside of Earlimart. Vignolo Farms owned the house and the few acres that surrounded it.

Al Stewart was a very good employee for many years. He worked hard during the work week; however, the weekend was a different story. It didn't take me long to find out Al Stewart had a problem with alcohol. We would sometimes see him roaming the streets in Earlimart on the weekends with a bottle of cheap wine in his back pocket. He was another person that I witnessed what consuming too much alcohol could do to a person. During the work week he was a stable human being. However, during the weekends, he was a drunk or what we would call a wino. He would sometimes come to Aunt Plute's house and drink with Uncle Cobb and Julius from across the street. I remember finding one of their bottles of cheap wine (white port) and unscrewing the top and taking a whiff. *Yuck, how could they drink this nasty s#it?* I thought. I promised myself that I would never allow myself to stoop so low that I would have to drink this stuff. All I can say about that last statement is that it was not the only promise that I made to myself that I would break during my lifetime.

I remember one day when Daddy and Al were spraying weeds at the South Ranch. They were driving a small tractor with a drum of weed-killing pesticide attached to it. It had a long rubber hose and a nozzle that was used for spraying the weeds. Of course I was outside watching them from a safe distance as they sprayed some weeds that were pretty close to our house. Daddy was driving the tractor, and Al was walking with the sprayer in his hand. Then all of a sudden, all hell broke loose. The hose from the weed-killer pump suddenly burst, thus spraying the dangerous pesticide everywhere. Daddy, who was still on the tractor, managed to avoid the calamity. I wish that I could say the same for Al Stewart. He was drenched from head to toe with that foul-smelling weed killer. Daddy immediately jumped off the tractor to come to his rescue. Al, with the weed killer still dripping from his face, assured Daddy that he would be okay. Daddy pleaded to him that he had better call someone to take him to the doctor. Al was not having any of that. Al told Daddy that it was no big deal and that when he got home, he would just rub a little salve (black people's wonder drug at the time) on his skin.

However, Daddy was able to convince Al that he should take the rest of the day off. Al agreed, and Daddy drove him back to his place. Daddy worried all night about how that weed killer would blister Al's skin. When Daddy went to work the next morning, he couldn't believe his eyes when the first person that he saw was a gregarious, skinny, dark-skinned, shiny-mouthed, dirty-joke-telling man that went by the name of Al Stewart. Daddy later told us that Al Stewart was indeed a "tough little toad."

One final thing about Al Stewart for now. As you may know by now, I have or will mention what I refer to as "man talk." It can be anything from telling dirty jokes, talking about sex, to discussing sports. It can sometimes go into deep stuff like astronomy, archaeology, or the latest stock price. Of course where I am from, it is definitely the former. As I said earlier, Al Stewart was a good human being. He never messed with anybody and was a friend to just about everyone. However, as I said earlier, truth be said, he was a drunk. It was just the way he chose to live his life.

Anyway, it was well-known at the South Ranch and all of the other ranches through man talk that Al Stewart was very well endowed. Now this is not the kind of endowment that comes from a family trust or some other financial institution. In other words (man talk) "the negro had a big d#ck." In fact, Daddy would sum up Al Stewart with one of his famous sayings. He would say that Al Stewart's situation was kind of sad. He said Al was a good example of "A million-dollar d#ck on a two-bit ass."

Lemuel Leffler

Lemuel Leffler was another man that I remember while growing up at the South Ranch. He was Daddy's boss. He was a white man that lived on one of Vignolo's ranches that was near Earlimart. Lemuel was married and had two kids, a boy and a girl. Since they were a few years older than I was, I never got to know them well. However, the son, Randy, would ride around the farms sometimes with his father. His wife was rarely seen as well.

Daddy really liked Lemuel and would always say that he was the best boss that he ever had. Lemuel treated all the workers fairly no matter what the color of their skin was. Lemuel was a very intelligent man that would later leave Vignolo Farms and start his own business.

C. J. Vignolo

C. J. Vignolo was of Italian descent and became one of the most successful farmers in the San Joaquin Valley. According to Daddy, he was a "people person extraordinaire." Ted would chop it up with his employees and refer to them as his family, thus ingratiating himself with his employees. He would always call Daddy "Son," which Daddy took to heart. Daddy believed that he was very privileged to be working for such an important person. He held Ted in the highest regard. He would brag to us about how his boss would buy a brand-new Cadillac Eldorado every year and dress up in the finest clothes. He would say that Ted Vignolo was rich as "sixteen foot up a bull's s#s". I never knew what he meant by that and still don't, but it sure sounded good. It was just another one of Daddy's Southern country boy sayings.

Bob Vignolo

Bob Vignolo was the only son of C. J. "Ted" Vignolo. He was a graduate of UC Davis and was courted by his father to be the "heir apparent" of the Vignolo Farm empire. Daddy would always tell me how sometimes Bob would confide in him when Ted would berate him publicly on the radio call system for making bad decisions. Under Ted's helm, Bob would become a feared and hated boss by many of the farm workers. It was kind of sad because Bob was actually a very good guy who was only trying to please his demanding father. Whenever word would get out that Bob was in the area, workers would tense up knowing that Bob would be on the rampage. Bob did not have the natural people skills and charisma that his father was blessed with. All Bob knew was to push his employees at all costs through fear. That's the way he was taught, so that's all he knew. Bob was a hands-on type that would walk the muddy cotton and grape fields in his worn-out boots. Bob would also get a new car every year, but like his personality, his car of choice was the exact opposite of his father's. He would usually get a new Chevrolet Malibu, Monte Carlo, or something similar.

Daddy and the other workers would look on in disbelief as Bob would get back into his new car with his boots covered in mud. Before long that shiny new car (which any of the workers would love to have) would be a dirty and filthy mess inside and out. Bob would never wash it because a new car didn't mean anything to him except a means of transportation. At the time, along with Daddy and the other workers, I couldn't understand how someone like Bob could disregard something like a new automobile as a tool for his work. Today, I understand perfectly why he did what he did. In a multi-million dollar business like they had, a car was just a tool. We were always looking at Bob through a "poor man's lens," which meant that we were totally blind and would never understand his situation. However, I am happy to say, unlike Daddy and the other workers, "T'was blind but now I see."

Dr. Pepper Man

I just wanted to spend a little time right now discussing how we did not grow up with alcohol directly affecting our family at the South Ranch. Although we would see it in other places like Teviston, Earlimart, and Bakersfield, we didn't see it at home. The reason was that Mama and Daddy did not drink. Daddy was known as the Dr. Pepper Man because he would drink Dr. Pepper just about every day. Looking back, drinking soda just about every day was probably not good for him, but it was surely better than drinking White Port, Thunderbird, or Night Train. It was a treat for us kids because most of the time, he would just drink about half of the bottle and leave it in his car. Of course this meant open season for thirsty little "soda pop gremlins."

It was first come, first serve, so we kept a keen eye on Daddy's car as he got off work and approached the South Ranch. The great thing about scoring the Dr. Pepper was not only quenching our parched throats but we would also "double dip," meaning that we would get to keep the five cents for the bottle as well. I remember some of us kids lining our bottles up on the window ledges on the back porch of the house. We couldn't wait for the next trip to Earlimart to cash our bottles in to buy, you guessed it, more soda. I wish I could say that Daddy was a Dr. Pepper Man for the rest of his life, but unfortunately, I can't. In future chapters, I will explain how alcohol finally got its slimy tentacles around members of our immediate family and our outside family, including yours truly.

I would like to finish volume 1 of *Black Boy from the Barrio* with a story pertaining to a subject in which I started in the beginning of this book. In the dedication to my mother, I mentioned how she has struggled with mental illness all of her life. The following is a short story that will give you guys an idea of what it was like during some of the tough times in my younger life where I experienced mental illness firsthand. By telling this story, hopefully it will resonate with some people and help with the healing process. I know it did for me.

Finally, I would like to thank you guys who have read these stories and have supported me and my cause. I am forever grateful. Volume 2 will be released in the not-too-distant future. Some of the short stories will include "Starting Grade School," "Encounters with Death," "Gun Violence in the Hood," "Tough Boys in the Hood," "Sammy vs. Jessie," and plenty of more stories of the South Ranch as well as 1008 Oak Street. Again, thank you for your support and your interest. Way to go, guys!

Sincerely,
Neo

MAMA, ARE YOU OKAY?

Most of the things that went on at the South Ranch when I was a kid were fun and not very serious. I have a good sense of humor and like for my stories to have some satirical value whenever I can. However, some of the stories will be told in a way that will hopefully make you guys understand that life is hard to understand sometimes. This is a story that I would like to share because by telling it, hopefully, it can be used in a way that will help people in the healing process of their various mental illnesses. It is definitely therapeutic for me just by writing this untold story. Thank you, and I hope this short story will resonate with you in a positive way.

I got my first glimpse of mental illness when I was about eight or nine years old. It was during a typical summer at the South Ranch. My cousin Freida Smith was visiting us from their ranch in Teviston. She, Lulu, and I were playing outside like we usually did. Baylo called out to us because she wanted to show us something. As we curiously walked over to the side of the house where she was standing, she told us that she had a trick that she wanted to show us. I didn't have any idea what kind of trick that she was about to show us, but I did notice that a match would be involved.

Baylo had a one-gallon empty plastic container that Daddy would use to pour gasoline into the lawn mower. Lighting matches was not unusual for us kids at the South Ranch. We would use them to light the living room heater, light the burners on the stove, and burn the trash. We knew the dangers of playing with matches; however, it was never a problem because we practiced a lot of caution when using them.

Baylo held the jug in one hand and the match in the other. She lit the match by striking it against the wood siding of the house.

She threw the match directly into the empty jug. Unbeknownst to all of us, there was apparently some gasoline fumes in that plastic container. As soon as the match hit the bottom of the jug, a fireball shot up from the mouth of the jug, hitting Baylo squarely in the face. Baylo immediately started crying and worked feverishly to stop the flames. She succeeded as the flames went out very quickly. However, the flames singed her entire face. She had first-degree burns, which were not that serious. I think that it spooked her more than anything else.

Her eyelashes, eyebrows, and hair were slightly burned, but the most telling symptom from the flashburn was that her skin turned very dark in color. We immediately told her to come inside the house where someone could take a look at it. Terry, Wanda, and Netta were inside the house probably listening to some of the latest music on the record player. As they saw Baylo, they immediately got out the wonder drug of (you guessed it) salve. Netta spread it on Baylo's face, and it seemed to temper the burns very quickly. We realized that she would be okay, thank God!

During the time that all this drama was unfolding at the South Ranch, Mama and Daddy were in Earlimart running some errands. We were all inside the house attending to and comforting Baylo. Before long, we could hear the tires of the car running over the dirt and gravel that was in the driveway. We knew that Mama and Daddy were home. We also knew that this would not be a typical greeting. In fact, far from it. How do young kids tell their mother and father that their daughter came seriously close to being badly burned? You try to act as normal as possible, that's how. So everybody except Baylo went outside to the front yard to greet our parents. We made sure that Baylo should stay in the house so Mama and Daddy wouldn't jump to any conclusions when they saw her burned face. I wish that I could say that Mama and Daddy didn't jump to any conclusions, but I would be lying. While meeting them halfway in the yard and in the best way we could, we tried to explain to Mama and Daddy what had taken place while they were gone.

As several of us kids started to babble all at once, Mama and Daddy started to get a little nervous. Daddy told all of us to shut up and just let Netta explain what was happening. A teary-eyed Netta started to explain to Mama and Daddy what had happened. Like an attorney (Perry Mason in those days), she was flawless in her delivery of the matter at hand. Her first words were "Don't worry, it's not so bad." She was hoping that this would put them in a relaxed state before they saw Baylo. I must say that it was a great strategy on her part and she almost pulled it off until, of course, they saw Baylo.

Baylo came out of the house last wearing a white towel on her head that Netta had soaked in water to cool the burns. Daddy saw Baylo first and asked what had happened. When we told him, he looked at Baylo and agreed that the burns were indeed not serious. He looked closely at the shiny salve that was all over her darkened face and took a sigh of relief. He also told Baylo that that was not a very smart thing to do and he hoped that she had learned her lesson. Baylo nodded her head in agreement and realized how lucky she was and how she had narrowly escaped disaster. If there had been a "spider leg" (country talk for a little amount) of gas in that bottle, it could have ignited, thus catching her whole face on fire. However, that was not the case. So all was well, or so we thought.

We quickly found out that Mama's and Daddy's reaction to this little mishap couldn't be more different. Daddy shrugged it off calmly and thought nothing more about it. Mama, on the other hand, saw that Baylo's face was burned and immediately went into a full-blown panic attack. This was the first time that any of us kids saw Mama completely lose control. We didn't know about her prior nervous breakdowns or that she even had a problem at all. However, Daddy knew all too well. Apparently, she suffered a nervous breakdown while carrying me in her womb. Daddy didn't tell me until I was well into my twenties. I will discuss this important subject in very close detail in later chapters.

When Mama got a close-up look at Baylo's face, she immediately started to yell at the top of her voice, "Wanda did it! Wanda did it!" I believe that she blamed Wanda because Wanda was the most mischievous of us kids, like I was saying before, mainly because of her ongoing battles with Terry. I look back now and realize that we were all just kids playing our roles in the structure of a common family. So no one was to blame.

Mama started whaling her arms around uncontrollably and pointing her finger directly at Wanda. Daddy intervened and grabbed her shoulder, fearing that she might try to attack Wanda. For the first time in our lives, we were all witnessing a person having a nervous breakdown. This was very hard to watch because it was not just a random person, it was our beloved Mama, which made it truly disturbing.

As Daddy tried to calm her down, we all stood there in shock as she continued her rant. As I became an adult, Daddy told me about Mama's various nervous breakdowns during their marriage. Daddy explained to me (as we all saw that day) that whenever Mama would have a breakdown, she would get very restless and very anxious. She would get an incredible boost of energy that would make her want to walk anywhere and everywhere.

After trying to soothe her in any way that he could, Mama starting walking southbound on the side of Road 144. Her eyes were wide and she looked terrified. It was hard to watch back then as it is hard to write about it now. My eyes are starting to well up a little, but I want to finish this important story (and others) because I think that it can have a positive impact on not just our immediate family but perhaps also the lives of countless other people that suffer from mental illnesses as well, including me.

Daddy, who was mostly known for his inner strength and being a role model for us kids, was actually at a loss for words. He actually asked us what he should do about Mama. Having gone through this before, he realized that he had two options. One was to drive the car a half mile to try to pick her up. Or two, call the police. After all of us kids just shrugged our shoulders with the "I don't know" gesture, Daddy decided to take matters into his own hands and do the latter, which was to call the police. By the time the police arrived, Mama was probably about three miles south of the South Ranch and getting close to Delano. Daddy drove down to meet her about the same time the police arrived. Daddy would later tell us that the police officers had to restrain her and put her in handcuffs. While all of us kids were still standing in the front yard, a police car pulled into the driveway. Daddy was right behind them in his yellow '64 Chevy Impala.

It was very sobering and very sad to see Mama in the back of that squad car. It was as if she was a criminal or something riding in the back seat with the steel barrier separating her from the police officers. Daddy got out of his car and approached the police car and started talking to the officers. As we kids kept our distance, we could see that Daddy was being asked by the police if he thought if they should release her. While looking at Mama and having been in this situation before, Daddy knew it would be best if they took her. He reluctantly told the officers what he thought was the best for her and the family at that particular time. The officers agreed, and off they went.

Mama had somewhat calmed down by the time she got back to the South Ranch; however, she still had a lot of nervous energy and could barely remain still. She looked at our saddened faces as the police car left out of the driveway. We watched as they headed north-bound on Road 144 until the police car and Mama disappeared. We wondered, "Where are they taking her?" Daddy, while still visibly upset about the whole occurrence, said that they were taking her to Stockton. "Stockton?" we said. Why Stockton? He said that Stockton was the place where they kept people that were mentally ill. We also asked how long would she be gone. Daddy said that he didn't know.

While still standing in the yard, Geraldine came to pick Freida up and take her home. Geraldine could visibly see that something was not right. She was used to seeing us kids joyfully playing games like we usually did. She asked Freida what was wrong. As humans, there are certain things that stick in our minds forever. This was one of those times for me. To this day, I can still vividly see Freida trying to explain to her mother what had happened. Freida just shrugged her shoulders and said, "I don't know. She just went crazy".

In future chapters I will go into further detail about Mama's lifetime battle with a serious mental illness and how she and Daddy managed to stay together and keep a family of seven children in an environment in which I consider a good upbringing. Way to go, Mama and Daddy!

EPILOGUE

I would like to thank you guys who have read these stories and have supported me and my cause. I am forever grateful. Volume 2 will be released in the not-too-distant future. Some of the short stories will include *Starting Grade School, Gun Violence in the Hood, Tough Boyz n the Hood, Sammy vs. Jessie,* and plenty of more stories of the South Ranch as well as 1008 Oak Street. Again, thank you for your support and your interest. Way to go, guys!

Sincerely,
Neo

CHARACTER REFERENCE

1. *Dorothy "June" Burton*, my mother.
2. *June Bug*, Aunt Plute's oldest son.
3. *Geraldine Bradford*, Aunt Plute's oldest daughter. She would later marry Freddie Smith. They had three kids. Their names were Randy, Raymond, and Frieda.
4. *James Bradford*, Aunt Plute's third oldest son.
5. *Curlee Bradford*, Aunt Plute's second oldest son. He was married to Wilma. They had three daughters. Their names were Traci, Leslie, and Gabby.
6. *Bruce and Mattie Burton*, the parents of my mother. They had sixteen kids. I will try to name some of them. Lena, Willie May, Shirley May, Arthur, Helen, Moses, Eugene, Wilbur, Bessie, Tony, and Dorothy. Sorry, I tried my best!
7. *Aunt Honey*, married to Uncle Booney. Their kids were: Frankie, Ruthy, Darnell, Shirley, Brenda, Debra, Ronald Gene, Kenny, and Stan.
8. *Clemetie "Bew" Wright*, my father.
9. *Aunt Tit* (a.k.a. Willie May), the oldest daughter of Mama Tina and Daddy Wright. She was married to Q. T. Hooks. They had two children, Roy and Lois.
10. *Uncle Q. T.*, married to Aunt Tit.
11. *Daddy Wright*, my dad's father. He was married to Christina Wright, a.k.a., Mama Tina.
12. *Sonny and Clarice Perry*, friends of the Wright family. Sonny was one of Daddy's best friends. Some of their kids were named Joyce, Delores, Eloise, Lester, Tommy Joe, Martha Ann, and Cynthia.
13. *Lemuel Leffler*, Daddy's foreman.

14. *Aunt Plute*, the second oldest daughter of Mama Tina and Daddy Wright. She was married to Willie Bradford then to Harold Cobb. Her children were named Curlee, June Bug, James, Geraldine, and Halean.

15. *Cesar J Vignolo*, owner, founder, and CEO of Vignolo Farms. Vignolo Farms was one of the biggest farming businesses in the Central Valley. He had a son named Bob.

16. *Blanche Gibson*, Mama's best friend. They met at an institution for the mentally ill. Blanche's kids were very close to our family. Their names were Wanda Mae, Quentin, Lillie Pearl, and Jeannie.

17. *Uncle Booney (a.k.a. Frank)*, the oldest son of Mama Tina and Daddy Wright.

18. *Mama Tina*, my grandmother on my father's side of the family. Her real name is Christina Wright. She was married to Willie Wright.

19. *Jack and Marilee Wells*, friends of the Wright family. Jack was one of Daddy's best friends.

20. *Manuel Gutierrez*, Daddy's workmate. He and his family lived at the North Ranch, which was about three miles from the South Ranch. He spent most of his time working at the South Ranch.

21. *Walter and Verdell Freeman*, friends of our family who lived in Teviston. We were very close with their children while growing up. In fact, my sister, Netta, would marry one of the Freeman boys named Michael. Some of their kids were named Jewell, Bug, Sandra, Michael, Ronald, Donald, Benny, and Janice.

22. *Al "good kid" Stewart*, Daddy's friend and workmate.

ABOUT THE AUTHOR

Cornelius "Neo" Wright is a certified life coach, author, speaker, and philanthropist. After twenty-five years of being in "the desert of life," he has just recently found out his true meaning of his existence. Through faith, hope, failure, and pure determination, he has reached a point in his life where he can look back in retrospect and see why he was *chosen* to live this particular life. One of his favorite quotes is "The two most important days of your life are (1) the day you were born and (2) the day you found out *why* you were born." Please join him on this exciting journey of him finding his *why*. And who knows? You might find your *why* as well.

Printed by BoD™in Norderstedt, Germany